AMISH SUMMER
OF COURAGE

Book Six
Jacob's Daughter series

WRITTEN BY
Samantha Jillian Bayarr

PRINTED IN THE UNITED STATES

Livingston Hall Publishers
Samantha Jillian Bayarr
Book SIX of Jacob's Daughter series

Also by Samantha Jillian Bayarr

LWF Amish Series
Little Wild Flower Book I
Little Wild Flower Book II
The Taming of a Wild Flower
Little Wild Flower in Bloom
Little Wild Flower's Journey

Christian Romance
Milk Maid in Heaven
The Anniversary

Christian Historical Romance
A Sheriff's Legacy: Book One
Preacher Outlaw: Book Two
Cattle Rustler in Petticoats: Book Three

Jacob's Daughter Amish Collection
Jacob's Daughter
Amish Winter Wonderland
Under the Mulberry Tree
Amish Winter of Promises
Chasing Fireflies
Amish Summer of Courage
An Amish Harvest
An Amish Christmas Wish

Companion Series
An Amish Courtship
The Quilter's Son
An Amish Widower
Amish Sisters

Please note: All editions may not be available yet.
Please check online for availability.

CHAPTER 1

"Don't scream!"

Rachel couldn't breathe.

The cold hand clenching her mouth was making it impossible for her to take in air. Panic seized her as she tried to wriggle free, but the *mann's* grasp on her was too strong.

"If you scream, I'm gonna have to hurt you."

He was behind her, and she couldn't see his face, but she could smell his sour breath on the back of her neck. It was enough to make her want to vomit. His free hand worked quickly, winding thin rope around her wrists so tight her hands were going numb.

What's happening to me? Gott, please help me!

Tears filled Rachel's eyes as the stranger tied her wrists tightly behind her back. She couldn't move even if she wanted to; her legs felt like silos filled to the brim with thousands of pounds of grain.

The bakery had closed for the day, and she had stayed longer than she should have washing dishes that should have been done during her down-time after the noon rush. It was nearly dark, but even at this late hour, no one was expecting her at home. It was Saturday, and she always made deliveries on her way home, distributing leftover bread to members of the community who were struggling. By the time her deliveries were missed, it would be too late for anyone to help her. Was he going to kill her? Was he here to rob the cash drawer? She would gladly give him all the money she had if he would let her go. But how could she tell him this?

She tried talking around the hand that covered her mouth, but the words came out muffled and unrecognizable.

He tightened his grip on her. "I'll be taking the money you have here, but it's not enough. Your sister knows where there's more, and I aim to get it—in exchange for you."

His hand dug into the flesh on her cheeks, causing her pain. He let a mean-spirited chuckle escape his lips as he forced her down onto a chair. Keeping his hand over her mouth, he leaned down and wrapped the rope around her ankles, binding her tightly. Rachel watched with unseeing eyes as he masterfully bound her with only one hand.

He thinks my family has money to pay—a ransom? I'm being abducted! Gott, please make him let me go without hurting me!

After tying her ankles, he reached into his pocket and pulled out a roll of thick, gray tape. "I'm going to take my hand off your mouth for just a minute so I can put tape across your mouth. If you scream, I'm gonna have to hurt you. Do you understand that?"

Rachel nodded her head. He slowly moved in front of her, his head down. He was wearing Plain clothes and a straw hat. But no Amish *mann* would do harm to another like this.

"Who are you? And what do you want?" Rachel managed before he clamped his hand back onto her mouth.

Slowly lifting his head, she looked into his bloodshot eyes. Either he was *not* Amish, or he wasn't from around here.

"I'm here for my million dollars and I ain't leaving until I get my money. You're my insurance policy. Now shut up or I'll have to get out my gun. I know you don't want that." He gritted deeply stained teeth at her.

Rachel shook her head, her breath heaving through the fingers that clenched her mouth. Tears had blurred her vision, but there was something almost familiar about this *mann* that threatened her.

Rachel watched in horror as he stretched out a piece of tape from the roll. The screeching sound it made sent shivers through her.

"Please don't put that on my mouth. I won't be able to breathe. I promise I'll be quiet." Rachel begged.

The stranger grinned, showing his yellowed teeth. "That's what they all say."

Rachel's heart slammed against her chest wall. Had he done this before? Did he let them go, or did they *die?* It was too scary to think about.

There has to be a way out of this.

He stretched the tape across her face and smoothed it over her mouth with his hand. There was no one around even if she *could* scream, and no one was expecting her home until later. She tried not to cry anymore, knowing her nose was already too stuffed up to breathe well. It was a task to pull air in and out of her swollen nostrils, and she felt dizzy from the effort.

The stranger left her in the chair while he went to the front of the bakery. If she stood up, would she make it to the back door and into her buggy before he could get back? But how would she drive? Before she had any more time to think about it, he was back and looking her right in the eye.

Rachel blurred her vision, not wanting to see the evil in his eyes. He yanked her to her feet, pulling her close to him. "Let's go. It's gonna take forever to get back into town with that horse of yours."

That was his plan? To abduct her using her own buggy? No wonder he wore Plain clothes. It was a disguise so no one would notice him even if they rode right past him.

He turned her around to face him. "I don't want you to make any noise when we leave here or I'll have to get out my gun."

Rachel's eyes bulged as she looked at him closely for the first time. The long scar on his cheek was familiar. With a rush of thought, she remembered where she'd seen this *mann* before, and it made her sick to her stomach. She had been so foolish, so trusting. This *mann,* her abductor, had been in the bakery last month—with Levi.

CHAPTER 2

One month earlier...

Rachel had just put the last loaves of bread into the oven when she heard the jingling of the bells on the front door to the bakery.

It's a little early for a customer.

As she rounded the corner, her heart fluttered at the sight of the handsome stranger. Though Amish, she could tell he wasn't from her community, even if she had known him.

He smiled brightly, exposing dimples in each cheek. He tipped his black hat, leaving it securely on his head that was full of thick, blond hair.

"Gudemariye. Wie gehts?" he almost seemed to struggle with the words, but Rachel was too busy admiring his amber eyes that seemed to twinkle when he smiled. His Plain suit was a little too big for him, but she'd seen that many times in the community when an older sibling passed on clothing to the younger ones. She guessed him to be around eighteen years old.

He held out a soft hand to Rachel and she took it. Most Amish *menner* had calloused hands by the time they reached the age of five. Why didn't he?

"I'm Levi Schrock. I'm looking for Hiram Miller's place."

"You came to the right place. I'm Rachel, and he's *mei grossdaddi*. Are you the one he hired to help bring in the harvest?"

"*Jah,*" he said.

Rachel tipped her head to one side. "He isn't expecting you for at least another month."

"*Jah, mei daed* sent me a little early, hoping I could earn some extra money. It's just the two of us, and we rent a little place in town with no land. I will send most of my earnings back home to Ohio to cover the rent. He's getting on in years and can no longer work."

Again, his accent was off, and his story sounded almost rehearsed. Rachel ignored the gentle nagging in the back of her mind. He was handsome, and a stranger. What more could a girl who was bored with the locals ask for?

"I'm sorry to hear that. I'm sure there will be plenty of work to keep you busy until the harvest. You aren't far from his farm. If you go out of the bakery and walk across the road and down to the left, you will reach his farm."

For a fleeting moment, she thought she'd seen him in the bakery a few days before, but the *mann* she'd seen had not been Amish.

Rachel sized him up. "You look familiar. Have I seen you in here before?"

"*Nee,* this is my first trip to your community."

Levi shifted the knapsack hanging from his shoulder, and pointed his nose toward the display case behind Rachel. "How about I get some of those cookies before I go? I could use something sweet."

He winked and Rachel blushed. She'd never been winked at before, but the Amish boys in the area weren't real big on flirting. She moved behind the counter and opened the display case.

She smiled at Levi. "How many would you like?"

"If they're half as sweet as you, Rachel, you better give me only a few. A fella can only handle so much sweet stuff until he gets addicted and wants more."

"I've been told my cookies are very addictive, so you come back for more any time you like."

Rachel was surprised by her own forwardness, but Levi didn't seem to mind. His smile told her he had enjoyed every flirtatious word.

CHAPTER 3

Rachel watched the handsome stranger walk out the door of the bakery and head in the direction she had sent him. Part of her wanted to close the bakery and go with him. She would definitely be taking an extra loaf of bread to her *grossdaddi's haus* after work, and hopefully she would get an invite to have dinner with him, Nettie, and Levi.

જીભ્સૅ

When he was clearly out of view of the bakery, Levi pulled a cell phone out of his knapsack to call Bruce, his *dad*. He knew Bruce would be pleased that he'd already made fast friends with Rachel Yoder. He wouldn't dare tell Bruce he'd found her attractive and would enjoy dating her without the deceit. If this job was going to be as easy as he now thought, he would be rid of his dad and all the abuse that came with him before too long. He would take his cut of the money Bruce promised him, and then he'd leave without looking back. The sooner he could get the information on the whereabouts of the money Uncle Eddie had stashed just before he died, the sooner he would be a free man. With his eighteenth birthday just around the corner, he was more eager than ever to pull off the last job he would ever do for his dad. He never liked the stealing or the lying, and very soon he wouldn't have to anymore.

Unlike Bruce, Levi had a conscience. That had to count for something, and he didn't plan on entering into adulthood following in his father's footsteps. At eighteen, he would no longer have to obey his dad, and he would be free to make his own choices…the choices of the righteous man he wanted more than anything to be.

ॐ

Rachel looked at the clock for the hundredth time in the past hour. She'd been washing pans and bowls for the past forty-five minutes and hadn't had a single customer during that time. Tempted to lock the door and close for the day, Rachel forced herself to wash dishes until the last utensil was clean. After wiping down the surfaces, she hung up her apron, feeling a sense of accomplishment. She was almost too tired to pay a visit to her *grossdaddi*, but she was too eager to see Levi again to care.

Unable to wait any longer, Rachel locked the door to the bakery, two loaves of fresh bread tucked under her arm.

Heading toward her *grossdaddi's* farm, Rachel uttered a quick prayer that Levi was able to secure work the way she'd half-promised him he would. If he wasn't, and he'd had to leave, there was no telling if he'd return for a second trip later in the season. She didn't like the idea of not finding the handsome newcomer at the farm. But if he wasn't there, he'd be long-gone by this time, and she'd be lucky to ever lay eyes on him again.

CHAPTER 4

Nettie welcomed Rachel with a smile. "*Danki* for the bread. It will make a *gut* addition to the meal tonight. I was hoping to make something light this evening since it's so warm; now we can have cold meat sandwiches. Would you like to join us?"

"*Danki*, I'm very hungry after working all day. Where's *mei grossdaddi?*"

Nettie set the bread on the counter and began washing a few tomatoes. "He's in the barn with the new hired hand. He arrived early from Ohio hoping to find work sooner than the harvest. Hiram didn't waste any time putting him right to work."

Rachel was delighted to hear that Levi had indeed been hired on and would be spending the next few months in the community. She felt that would be plenty of time to get to know him better. Her heart fluttered at the possibility of courting Levi. Surely he wouldn't be here if he was betrothed back in his own community.

Nettie cut up lettuce and tomatoes for the sandwiches, while Rachel sliced cheese from the large block that her *grossdaddi* made. He sold the cheese to others in the community after curing it in the barn, but it was more of a hobby than a source of income, she thought.

"Go ahead and ring the bell. I'll finish putting out the pickled beets and cold potato salad I made earlier."

Suddenly feeling a little nervous, Rachel stepped outside and pulled the string, clanging the bell to alert her *grossdaddi* and Levi. She didn't stay outside to wait for them. Instead, she quickly returned to the kitchen to busy her hands with setting the table. Hopefully, they would take a few minutes to come in from the barn, allowing Rachel enough time to steady her nerves.

All too soon, Rachel heard the back door swing open, and the sound of male voices. She kept her back to them as she finished stirring up a pitcher of grape Kool-Aid.

She felt an arm go around her shoulder. "It's *gut* to see you, Rachel." Hiram said.

Rachel stopped what she was doing and hugged him back. "You smell like cheddar cheese, *grossdaddi.*"

"I've got two milk cows that give us more milk than we can possibly use. I'll be making some butter this week too, if you need some for the bakery."

"*Danki,* my supply is starting to run a little low."

Hiram chuckled. "I had a feeling it might be. Let's eat. I'm hungry as a horse."

Up until this point, Rachel had avoided seeing Levi, though she knew he was just a few feet behind her. Luckily, they sat very quickly and bowed their heads for the silent prayer. She hadn't dared look at him for fear her *familye* would see the blush that already tried to creep up her neck.

Dear Gott, please keep my nerves steady, and don't let me make a dummkopf of myself in front of Levi. Oh, and please bless this food and my familye.

When she heard the clanging of silverware, Rachel lifted her eyes to Levi, who sat staring at her. Had he been watching her the whole time? She fidgeted a little in her chair until she noticed her *grossdaddi* slapping a hand on his shoulder.

"This is Levi Schrock. He'll be helping me until mid-October."

That long? That was nearly three months away. Rachel was pleased to hear it.

Levi felt funny being called by his friend's name from back in Ohio. When he'd stayed with the Schrock family over the previous summer while Bruce was in jail, he and Levi had become good friends. And now, here he was, using Levi's good name to deceive these people.

It's only for a little while so I can get away from Bruce. Then they will never see me again.

Levi nodded his head and smiled at Rachel, bringing heat to her cheeks. *"Jah,* we met this morning when I stopped at the bakery for directions."

Nettie nudged Rachel gently with her foot under the table, startling her. "Why didn't you tell me you already met him?"

Rachel's cheeks turned a deep shade of red at Nettie's question. What could she have said? That she'd met a really handsome, possible suitor, and she only came over to see *him?*

"I suppose it hadn't crossed my mind to mention it."

Nettie looked at her knowingly, leaving Rachel feeling as though she'd lied to the woman. In a way, she had lied by way of omission of information, but she was of the mindset that what they didn't know couldn't hurt *her.*

Hiram placed another slab of ham on his bread, making his sandwich almost too thick to bite into. "I'll be having Levi make deliveries for me to save time, so he'll bring the butter over to the bakery on Thursday. I think I'm going to like having a hired hand. We might just have to negotiate an extended stay for you, Levi. Already my mind is awhirl over everything from chopping wood and shoveling snow, to making candles and sheering the sheep. I don't know why I've been trying to do everything myself this year. Since Seth got married, I've been trying to shoulder all the work on my own." He slapped Levi on the shoulder. "Now I may not have to. We got more done today than I have in the last week."

Levi smiled, catching Rachel's eyes. She was happy to hear that it was working well for him to help—if it meant he might stay in the community. But then a thought hit her like a rock.

"What about your *daed,* Levi? Won't he miss you being gone all this time?"

How could he have a chance to miss me when he got himself a room in the motel in town so he could keep an eye on me until I get him the stolen money?

Levi shrugged. He shoved a forkful of potato salad into his mouth, keeping his eyes on his plate.

It was obvious to everyone at the table that Levi didn't want to answer that question. She knew firsthand that every *familye* had its struggles, but Levi almost seemed like he was hiding something. Perhaps he was younger than she'd originally thought, and he'd run away from home. He hadn't mentioned his *mamm,* but spoke only of his *daed.* She noticed a sense of sadness about him that he was trying hard to cover. But his eyes gave him away; those sad, amber eyes.

CHAPTER 5

During the meal, Levi felt Rachel's eyes on him, but he tried to steer the conversation to his new duties at the Miller farm, hoping she wouldn't catch his mishaps. If he didn't start keeping track of his lies, he would blow his cover, and she would never trust him enough to confide in him. He also needed to keep her interest to allow him the opportunity to talk to her sister, Abby. Knowing Abby was married, he would not be able to talk to her unless in the company of Rachel, so she would be the perfect go-between. He hated the deception, especially since this family had already been so kind to him. And if he wasn't careful, he would end up falling for the beautiful Rachel, and that would interfere with his plan to be rid of his father once and for all.

The previous summer he'd spent at the Schrock farm had taught him a lot about the Amish culture. They were a kind and generous group of people, and he hated taking advantage of their pure goodness. He had learned that each community is different and has its own rules; however, one thing remained true in all of them—their kind and gentle nature. At the end of the summer, when Bruce had gotten out of jail, Levi hadn't wanted to leave the farm and return home.

His dad had been the one to suggest Levi pose as Amish to weave his way into their lives so he could get the information he needed to locate the stolen money. His dad had told him the money had sat long enough that the state of Ohio had probably forgotten all about it. He certainly hoped it was true since he didn't want to go to jail.

ℬℭ

Rachel climbed reluctantly into her *grossdaddi's* buggy; she couldn't believe he'd suggested so casually that Levi drive her home. As she nestled in next to Levi, Rachel blushed at the closeness.

Levi picked up the reins with shaky hands.

"I'm not the best driver. I've only driven a few times last summer when I helped my cousins on their farm. Since *mei Daed* and I have lived in town most of my life, we don't even have a horse."

"I can teach you the way *mei Daed* taught me when I was just a wee little girl."

Rachel placed her hands over the top of Levi's hands, guiding the reins to maneuver the horse. It amazed her at how soft his hands were. She supposed living in town instead of on a working farm would do that to a *mann's* hands. In time, she would see the callouses of a hard-working *mann*—especially if he continued to work for her *grossdaddi*. Hiram Miller had worked hard all his life, and he expected the same from those around him. Rachel had always admired that about him, though she'd heard from her *mamm* and *Onkel* Seth that he could be quite stern.

As they let the mare trot down the main stretch of road past the bakery, Rachel let go of Levi's hands and allowed him control. "I think you're getting the hang of it. Will you be alright by yourself on the way back?"

Levi smiled at her. "I think I will. *Danki* for trusting me."

Rachel smiled. "If *mei grossdaddi* trusts you, then I do too."

Maybe this job will be easier than I thought. If she trusts me enough to drive her home, surely she will get her sister to trust me with the secret of where that money is hidden. The sooner I get it back to Bruce, the sooner I can get on with my life. All I want to do is finish this job for Bruce and get out of here before I become too attached to this beautiful girl.

೮೦೧೩

Rachel allowed herself to bump into Levi every time the buggy hit a rut in the shoulder of the road. She didn't mind the contact with the handsome stranger who intrigued her with every story he told about his life in Ohio. Though he was only making small-talk now, she picked up subtle traces of inconsistencies in his tales. Not that she doubted he was from Ohio, or that he lived in town with his *daed;*

perhaps that was why he seemed more *Englisch* than Amish. She wondered if her *grossdaddi* had picked up the same clues in Levi's speech, or if he was so happy to have help that he didn't see past the strong pair of hands that eased his own workload.

"How long have you been without a *mamm?*"

Levi cleared his throat, pausing to choose his words carefully. "I honestly don't know. *Daed* told me a story, but I don't remember much about her. I haven't seen her since I was seven years old. She didn't live with us, but she visited. Then she stopped suddenly. I've not seen her since, and don't really remember her."

Rachel's heart thumped in her chest. She couldn't imagine not seeing her *mamm,* or knowing where she was. Her own *schweschder* had never seemed to display a void from losing her real father, but Levi held a cloud of sadness in his eyes when he spoke of his *mamm.* Was it possible that Abby felt the same at losing her *daed,* but pushed her feelings down? They'd never really talked about it. She knew he had been of undesirable character, but it was obvious that Levi's *mamm* was of questionable character as well.

"You should talk to my *schweschder.* She's had kind of the same problem in her life, except my *daed* became her *daed* when she was ten years old. I know it's too late for you to have a new *mamm,* but you both lost a parent around the same age. Maybe she could offer some advice on how she settled things in her heart."

Levi couldn't believe Rachel had just handed him the key to open the door of communication with her sister, Abby.

"*Jah,* it would be nice to speak to someone else who might understand what I've gone through. Losing a parent isn't easy, no matter what the circumstances. Did your *schweschder's daed* walk out on her too?"

"*Nee,* he died in a car accident. But he didn't know she was his *dochder.* They never knew each other."

Levi steered the buggy into the long drive leading to Rachel's *haus.* "But if she never knew him, what was there for her to settle? How can you feel a loss for something you never had?"

Rachel scrunched her brow. "I'm not sure. I suppose you will have to ask her yourself. *Danki* for the ride. I hope I will see you again soon."

Levi smiled. "You can count on it."

CHAPTER 6

"Why are you telling complete strangers my personal business?"

Rachel looked at her *schweschder* across the counter of the bakery. Her arms were crossed over her chest and her eyes narrowed.

They exchanged Abby's order across the display case that was already emptying of the day's baking.

"He's not a complete stranger; he's living with Nettie and *Grossdaddi.*"

Abby rolled her eyes. "That's no testament of a *mann's* character. *Grossdaddi* would take in a dozen prisoners if he thought he could rehabilitate them. He told you he was from the community near where *mamm* and I used to live. How do we know that Eddie's friends aren't still out there somewhere hoping to collect on his debt? You know how quickly word gets around when people start wagging their tongues. If he wants to talk about loss in his life, that's one thing. But please don't talk about my past anymore. You know how hard *mamm* worked to keep all that a secret."

Rachel leaned across the counter. "Didn't her secrets almost destroy your chances of a normal life with Jonah?"

Abby scowled. "We are married now and that's all that matters. *Mamm* did what she thought she had to do in order to protect me. I know that now. I only hope that my connection with Eddie's *familye* hasn't jeopardized my future. I will always have that little bit of fear hanging over my head. Just be careful what you say to Levi. You never know what he could be putting in his letters back home."

Rachel agreed, though she didn't understand her *schweschder's* continued caution over the subject. Eddie had been gone since Abby was ten years old.

৪৩০৪

Hiram pulled the bucket up from the well and splashed the earth-cooled water on his face. He had gotten too warm again and run out of energy. His back ached, and his joints stiffened. Levi was a hard worker, so why was he still pushing himself as though he were still a young *mann?* The doctor had told him to take it easy, but he feared if he sat around he would feel useless. His sons had farms of their own and had no use with his. Who would even inherit his property when he was gone? Hiram shook the thought from his mind; he wasn't ready for *Gott* to take him yet. He was newly married, and it had made him young at heart again—hadn't it?

Feeling over-heated and sick from the heat of the sun burning his backside, Hiram stumbled over to the large oak tree in the yard and collapsed at the base.

Dear Gott, please don't make my Nettie a widow so soon.

Levi hadn't noticed when Hiram disappeared from the field where they'd been turning up the soil between rows of vegetables. When he saw his boss fall against the tree in the yard, he took off running toward him. When he reached the tree, he leaned against it, trying to catch his breath.

"Are you hurt?"

Hiram looked up at him with weak eyes that squinted against the bright afternoon sun. "I think the heat got to me. Let me rest a spell, and I'll be back in the field to help you."

Levi crouched down and leaned on his haunches. "Your entire shirt is soaked with sweat, and your face is beet-red."

Hiram waved him off with his hand. "I spilled water down the front of me when I pulled the bucket from the well. I'm probably just sunburned. I should be alright in a few minutes."

Levi wasn't convinced. "You sound out of breath. Should I get a doctor?"

Hiram tried to stand, but his legs were too shaky, and nausea consumed him. "Maybe you better go call Doctor Davis. The number is on the wall in the barn near the phone."

Levi didn't want to leave Hiram alone too long, so he ran to the barn as fast as he could.

Lord, please don't let my new boss die. Spare his life, and let the doctor get here in time.

Levi rushed back to Hiram after begging the doctor to hurry. "The doc said to get you out of the heat. Do you think you can walk if I help you?"

Hiram nodded.

"C'mon, let's get you inside."

Levi bent down and tucked his arm under Hiram's and helped him to his feet. Steadying him, Levi walked slowly to get him in through the kitchen door and set him down at the table. Hearing the commotion, Nettie rushed into the room.

"What happened?" She held a hand to her throat, her face ashen.

Levi began to unlace Hiram's work boots. "He got overheated. The doc said to get him inside and take his shoes off to cool him down. Could you bring him a drink of water? Doc said only tap water—nothing cold or it could throw him into shock."

Nettie had already gotten a glass out of the cupboard before he finished his sentence.

"The doc said he'd be here in a few minutes."

When he finished with Hiram's shoes and socks, Levi pulled his hat off his head and fanned Hiram's face with it.

Hiram snatched the hat from Levi's hand playfully. "Don't fuss over me. I'll be fine as long as I sit here for a minute and catch my breath."

Nettie placed the glass of water in her husband's hand. "Don't be so stubborn, old *mann;* the *buwe* was only doing what Doctor Davis told him to do. Now drink up."

Levi sat across from Hiram, feeling the danger of what could have happened to his boss if he hadn't noticed Hiram had left the field when he did. If anything had happened to his boss, he'd be out of a job and would have to go back home empty-handed.

Shame on me for thinking such selfish thoughts. Lord, forgive me for being so selfish. Please make Hiram well again; not for my sake, but for Nettie's.

CHAPTER 7

Doctor Davis put away his stethoscope and stood at the foot of the bed of his most stubborn patient.

"You rest now, Hiram. Heat stroke is no laughing matter." He turned to Nettie. "Don't let him out of that bed tomorrow."

Nettie smirked. "Now, Doc, you know that's not as easy as it sounds."

Hiram adjusted the pillow beneath his head. "I have to tend to my corn field."

Levi stepped in from the doorway where he'd remained while the doctor did his examination. "I can finish it. You get your rest."

Hiram shook his head in discouragement. "You know I can't afford to pay you more wages for doing my half of the work."

Levi looked at him sternly. "I can only work as fast as *one* man and can only do the work of *one* man. You will pay me the wages we already agreed upon; you can help when you're feeling better, or whenever the doc gives you the *okay*."

Hiram looked at Levi. He was an honest, hard-working young *mann,* but for the first time, Hiram noticed Levi spoke like an *Englischer.*

ଛୠ

Levi picked up the cell phone from the solar-powered charger he'd put in the window of his room at the Miller's house. Bruce had sent him several text messages asking for a progress report. He was tempted to ignore the messages, but he knew Bruce would come looking for him if he didn't stave him off with some sort of news. But what could he say without hurting Rachel or her family, and yet give his dad a sense of satisfaction that this trip was producing the results he'd sought?

"I got the job. Will meet the whole family at dinner on Saturday. Will know more then."

Levi hit *send* and turned off the phone before he could get a response. Levi wasn't in the mood for a confrontational text war with Bruce, and when he received his son's vague text message, it was sure to make him angry. Feeling the exhaustion from the long day he'd had in the field, he collapsed onto the soft bed and pulled the feather pillow under his weary head.

Lord, if you see fit to get me out of this mess somehow, I pray that you will rescue me from my own poor judgment. Please forgive me for deceiving these nice people.

ഇൗരു

Because of Hiram's heat stroke, the butter did not get made the day before. Now it was up to Levi to take over. Sadly, he had to admit that he'd never churned butter before. After a few quick instructions from Hiram to get started, Levi headed for the root cellar where a ten-gallon bucket full of fresh cream waited for him. How hard could it be to slosh it around a churn for a few minutes? He'd seen Mrs. Schrock churning butter on the front porch of the farm where he'd worked the previous summer, so he felt he had a basic understanding of it from watching the process. So how hard could it be?

With a churn full of cold cream, Levi settled in on the front porch where he could enjoy the summer breeze while he worked on the first batch. After about twenty minutes, his arms started to ache. He opened the lid on the churn to see that the cream had begun to thicken and separate. Feeling confident the process was nearing its end, Levi pushed through the pain, taking very short breaks to rest his arms.

Hearing the screen door squeak, Levi looked up to see Hiram making his way toward him with two glasses of lemonade. He sat down in the chair beside Levi and offered him one of the glasses.

Levi took the glass and gulped the entire thing. "*Danki*, that hit the spot."

Hiram cocked his brow. "I thought you could use a little break. How long have you been at it?"

Levi wiped sweat from his brow with the back of his hand. "Almost thirty minutes."

Hiram chuckled. "You're about halfway done. You want me to take a turn?"

Levi shook his head. "Doc said you were not to exert yourself. This is laborious work."

Hiram chuckle again. "Yes it is. It will give you some muscles."

Levi laughed. "I could stand to gain a bit of muscle."

"When you finish this part, I'll show you what the next step is."

Levi was grateful his boss was a patient man. He wished his own father could have been half as patient as Hiram, and a better example. Maybe then he wouldn't be here trying to deceive this man he admired. But maybe God wanted him here for a reason. Maybe he was meant to come here and learn to be a better man from this family. If anyone could teach him to be a better man, it was Hiram.

Then there was Rachel—beautiful Rachel, a girl he could see himself falling in love with. A girl he could see himself spending the rest of his life with. But who was he kidding? A girl like her would never want to be with him. Especially when she and her family discovered what kind of man he really was. He was a thief and a liar. Would they ever forgive him? Would God forgive him?

CHAPTER 8

By the time Levi finished straining and rinsing the last batch of butter, he wasn't sure his arms would ever work again. He had placed two pounds of the butter into wooden molds for the Millers to use; the rest was packed into plastic, reusable containers that would need to be delivered to the bakery immediately. Though Levi was much too tired to make the delivery, he was eager to see Rachel again.

He had never worked so hard in all his life. When he'd worked for the Schrock family the previous summer, they'd taken it easy on him, teasing him and saying that he was a soft *Englischer*. Today he didn't feel like that. Today, he felt he could pull his weight and more if needed, in order to prove his worth to his new employer—especially since Hiram believed him to be Amish. He had to put that *soft Englischer* behind him and tough it out. He knew the Amish worked hard, and he would pull his weight even if every muscle in his body protested.

Filling the back of the buggy with the tubs of butter, Levi set off on the short journey to the bakery before Rachel closed for the day. Hiram had told him that she would need the butter when she opened in the morning, and he didn't want to let either of them down. Steering the buggy down the main road, Levi remembered the softness of Rachel's hands when she'd wrapped them around his the other day. Using the method to give him a driving lesson had tickled his senses in a way no other female had ever come close to in his life. Driving was really a matter of a few simple commands, Levi had discovered, but the horse was so well-trained, the buggy practically drove itself. It still made him tingle at the thought of her hands resting on his.

When he pulled into the back of the bakery, he wasn't sure if he should go around to the front the way her customers did, or if he should risk frightening her by going in the back door. Stepping down, his body stiffened under the strain he'd put on his muscles. Moving was slow, and everything ached. Leaving the butter in the buggy, he decided it was best to go through the front door so he wouldn't startle her.

The jingling of the bells on the door rang in his ears as he opened the door, the strong smell of sweet baked goods filling the air. Levi's stomach gave a rumble, reminding him that he'd not eaten for many hours. He chuckled to himself knowing that hard work had made him that hungry.

Rachel was behind the counter and looked beyond the customer she was helping to flash Levi a smile. In that short moment of eye-contact with him, she'd thought he looked somehow different than he'd looked the day before. How had one day managed to change him? Truth be told, he looked more Amish than he had the first day she'd met him. Was it possible that living in the city instead of a farm had robbed him of his true heritage? Rachel could sense his eyes on her as she finished with the last customer for the day.

Levi stepped forward and managed a weak smile. "I have your butter in the back of Hiram's buggy. Shall I bring it in through the back door?"

Rachel nodded, noticing how worn out he looked. Her eyes followed him as he walked slowly out the door, his gait was that of a much older *mann*. She giggled, knowing he was probably sore from churning the butter. She walked through the bakery and unlocked the back door, swinging it open for him.

She could see he was moving slowly, so she went to the buggy to help bring in the butter. Looking in the back at all the tubs, she gasped.

"You and *mei grossdaddi* have been hard at work today."

Levi cleared his throat. "Hiram suffered from a bit of heat-stroke yesterday when we were working in the fields. The doc told him to rest for the next few days and he'll be good as new."

"Did you churn all this butter by yourself?"

Levi looked at her with tired eyes.

"Yep—er—*jah,*" he said.

Rachel ignored his change in speech. She could see why he walked like he had been out plowing all day.

"I would not have been able to churn that much butter in one day."

Levi looked at her with one raised eyebrow and a crooked smile that she thought made him look very handsome. "It was the first time I'd ever churned butter before. Is it supposed to take that long?"

Rachel giggled. "*Jah,* it does." She opened one of the containers and peeked inside. "It looks and smells heavenly, so you must have done it right. *Danki,* you did a *gut* thing helping *mei grossdaddi.* May I ride back with you so I can check on him?"

"Of course you can," Levi managed.

Looking into her hazel eyes made Levi want to be a better man. If he could, and she would accept him, he would become Amish for her. He admired the closeness of her family and the unconditional love they all seemed to have for others. Was he capable of such love? He thought it was possible, especially with someone like Rachel to love him in return. Her lifestyle was something he'd craved ever since he left the Schrock farm at the end of the previous summer. He'd learned so much from the family—even how to pray. But when he'd returned home to his dad, his life was once again filled with hatred and despair to the point he'd made a promise to himself to find a way out. He would finish this job for Bruce, and then he would be free to love and be loved the way God wanted him to.

CHAPTER 9

Levi lay awake on top of the handmade quilt in his room at the Miller's house. He'd turned off the cell phone without checking the messages from Bruce. He was certain they were full of venom as usual, but tonight he didn't want to think about anything except Rachel. He would deal with his dad tomorrow morning when he went into town to give him most of his first week of pay. Levi wasn't looking forward to seeing the man, and all he wanted to do now was have a pleasant night of sleep after such a full day of hard work. His muscles ached more than they ever had before, but all he could think about was wrapping his tired and worn-out arms around Rachel.

A warm breeze fluttered the sheer curtains at the open window. It reminded him of the way Rachel's hair had danced across the side of her face when he drove her home in the open buggy. Hiram had offered the smaller buggy to save the tired horse from too much of a workout at the end of a long day. Levi thought it resembled the courting buggies he'd seen while staying with the Schrock's. Remembering how badly he'd felt at the end of the summer when Bruce got out of jail and he had to return to the careless ways of his father, he was grateful to be once again among the Amish and their gentle ways. If he could, he would stay here for the rest of his life. But even he knew that wasn't a realistic thought.

Levi rolled over toward the window, listening to the crickets and watching fireflies glow along the grass down below. His life had never been better than it was when he was among the Amish. Was it possible that he could take his share of the lost money and buy himself some land here and continue to live among the Amish? What would happen when they discovered he wasn't Amish? Would they shun him? If he was careful, maybe they would never know.

ॐ

After the morning chores, Levi harnessed the small buggy and headed into town. He'd asked Hiram before he took the job if it would be okay for him to take his wages to the post office at the end of each week, and he'd consented after making a comment about how pleased he was that Levi was responsible enough to take care of his elderly father. If Hiram had known that he was taking the money to a greedy *Englischer,* he might not have been so impressed with him. Bruce wasn't so old that he couldn't earn an honest wage, but he had led a hard life being in and out of jail over the years and leaving his only son to fend for himself. Levi hadn't even stayed in school, and his peers were about to graduate high school without him.

Maybe I fit in here in more ways than one. The Amish rarely go to school past the eighth grade. At least none of them would ever call me dumb like my so-called friends did.

When he steered the horse onto the main road in town, his heart rate went into double-time as the small motel came into view at the end of the strip. This would be the first time he'd seen Bruce since he'd gone to live at the Miller's house, and he wasn't looking forward to seeing him.

No sooner did he pull the horse up in front of room 217, than Bruce came staggering out the door. He smelled of tobacco and whiskey, and looked like he was in need of a good bath. His peppered gray hair stood up on one end, and his clothing looked as if he'd slept in it.

Bruce rested his arm across the buggy and leaned in toward his son. "Well look at you, Blake. I almost didn't recognize my own boy in that get-up. You look like a real Amish."

"Be quiet or someone will hear you. My name is Levi, and you better remember that or you will blow our cover."

Bruce grabbed his son by the collar and pulled him close. "And you better remember to respect me, Boy, or you won't like what will happen to you."

Levi cringed under his dad's threat. The sour smell of whiskey on the man's breath made him sick to his stomach, and his heart raced remembering many such similar confrontations that didn't end well. He was too old to allow this man to bully him, but Bruce had turned him into a coward who cringed at the rise of his dad's voice alone.

Bruce tightened his grip on Levi's shirt. "You got some money for me, Boy?"

Levi jerked from Bruce's grasp and reached into his shirt pocket. He pulled out the bills and handed them to his father.

Bruce snatched them out of his hand and examined them momentarily. "Is this all that Amish farmer is paying you? You're not holding out on me are you, Boy?"

Levi gulped. Bruce would know if he was lying to him, but he needed to keep a little bit of money to himself so he could buy a few necessities. He couldn't let Hiram pay him wages and take care of his every need on top of that.

He took a step back. "I kept a few dollars for myself so I could buy a bottle of aspirin and a tube of toothpaste. They're working me pretty hard and I get sore."

Bruce shook the money at his son. "You're young. You'll bounce back without aspirin. This is barely enough to cover my expenses here. What am I supposed to use to buy food? I gotta eat. I bet those Amish folks are feeding you real good. Meanwhile, your old man is sitting here starving."

Levi wanted to yell at his dad. Tell him to stop wasting his money on whiskey and cigarettes, and to put in an honest day's work. But anything he could have said would have fallen on deaf ears. They'd argued it over many times before, and the outcome was always the same. He wouldn't give Bruce the opportunity to give him a sound lashing out here on the street. He hopped in the buggy and flicked the reins on the backside of the mare, pulling back a little to the left to get her to back up. Levi wished he'd driven a car to the motel so his get-away would be faster, but he'd managed to send a clear message to Bruce. All he wanted to do was leave this life behind and truly be Levi Schrock; he no longer wanted to be Blake Monroe.

If only it was that easy.

CHAPTER 10

When Levi returned to the Miller farm, Hiram was waiting for him in the barn.

"I decided I needed to work with you today since we will end our work day early to have a meal with my *dochder* and her *familye*. I was a little curious as to why you aren't doing things traditionally. I know each community does things a little differently, but some of the things you do seem a little off balance."

Levi's heart beat faster. Had he been found out before he was able to get any information for Bruce regarding the whereabouts of the money?

Think, Blake! How would Levi answer such a question?

"I've lived in town with my *daed* all my life. I only learned most of what I know from being around my cousins on their farm. Last summer, when my cousin broke his leg, I stayed with them and stepped in to do his chores. It wasn't easy since I had never lived on a farm before. I'm sorry if I'm doing some of it wrong, but I've had very little instruction and had to learn most of it on my own. Since my *aenti* is a widow, my *onkel* wasn't there to work with me.

Please show me what it is I've done wrong. I'd like to make it right."

Hiram put his hand to his beard and gave it a tug. There was something not quite right about Levi's story. He hated the idea of checking up on him, but perhaps a letter to the Bishop in Ohio was in order. He would send the letter as soon as possible and make sure there was not something that Levi was trying to hide. If he was hiding from an offense in his own community, he would not find refuge here. Bishop Troyer, though very lenient, would hold him accountable for whatever it was that Levi was hiding. Hiram hoped it was just his imagination and that there was nothing Levi was running from. It wasn't just his language, but his lack of skills over simple chores that made Hiram suspicious of him. As an Elder of the community, he had a duty to make sure Levi's story checked out.

"Why don't we start with you putting things back where you found them? Since you are obviously not used to working on a farm, I will tell you that being organized is the best way to save time. I appreciate you making the butter in my absence yesterday, but now I can't even find the churn."

Levi gulped. "I left it on the side of the barn where I rinsed it off. I left it to dry and forgot to put it away. I'm sorry."

Hiram held up the milking stool and showed Levi its broken leg. "You left this in the stall after milking and she trampled it. I had to fix the leg before the morning milking. You must be more responsible, Levi."

"I will, Sir. I give you my word."

Hiram already thought Levi was a hard worker and admired his polite manners. But he couldn't shake the look on the young *mann's* face when he'd talked to him just now. He could see fear in Levi's eyes. He had to wonder if he'd suffered a few too many lashings growing up. The sadness in his expression when he thought no one was looking was almost haunting.

Instructing Levi on the proper way to clean the horse stalls was the first priority on Hiram's list. Each taking a stall, Hiram gave Levi detailed instructions, which he followed to the letter. It did his heart good to see how dedicated the young *mann* was. He certainly earned every penny of his wages. But there was still something not quite right about his young hired hand. If only Hiram could narrow it down.

Levi worked silently beside his boss. He knew the more he spoke, the more opportunity that left for him to make a mistake and say the wrong thing. He was already worried that Hiram suspected he was an imposter. Why had he thought he could pull off such a scam? Surely the Amish can recognize one of their own. He'd heard stories of people trying to hide among the Amish when they were in some sort of trouble, but he'd never heard of the outcome. Had it ever been successfully done? With few phones in the community and no internet access, how would they ever find out he was an impostor? Unless he made a mistake big enough to cause them alarm, he didn't see any reason his plan couldn't work. He'd already managed to fool them. He would work hard, keep his mouth shut as much as possible, and his ears open for any clues to the whereabouts of the money. The money that would free him from all of his problems.

CHAPTER 11

Levi was exhausted, and no longer feeling up to having dinner with Hiram's family. But knowing Rachel would be there made him eager to wash his face and put on a clean shirt and trousers. Knowing it might afford him the opportunity to talk to Abby made him both apprehensive *and* eager. He was all for getting the information he needed so he could get Bruce off his back once and for all. The sooner he could find out what Abby knew about the money, the sooner he could be rid of Bruce.

Levi paused, reflecting on the simplicity of the room he'd been staying in. No place had ever felt more like home to him. Never before had so much been at stake as it was now. His entire future was riding on this one piece of information. If he couldn't get it, he had no idea what his future would hold. He hated the thought of following in his father's path of petty crime. He wanted freedom—from a future life filled with sorrow, and freedom from Bruce. He could not let his fear get in the way of what he had to do. He would be bold and get answers, even if it caused suspicion.

Hiram called from the base of the stairs, asking if he was ready to go. Nettie had made a casserole to take with them. The smell filled the house, making Levi's stomach growl with anticipation. He'd worked so hard the past few days, he was hungry constantly.

Fresh air and hard work will do that.

৪৩৫৩

The drive to the Yoder farm was pleasant and scenic, as was all the area. He loved the sounds of cows and other animals from neighboring farms, chicken's clucking filling in the silence of the ride. It would have seemed awkward to ride in the back of the buggy, except that he enjoyed the secure, family feeling it gave him. He wished he could have been raised in such a serene place, but his reality was far from this. People had told him the Amish were a backward people, slow in everything they did. He'd seen the opposite since he arrived a week ago. They didn't have modern conveniences, but their lifestyle was anything but slow. Everything they did had a purpose: to serve their families and the community. If Levi could have his way, he would never leave.

When the buggy stopped, Levi jumped out of the back and assisted Nettie with her casserole. Rachel stood on the front porch wiping her brow with a tea-towel. She leaned against the rail and waved to everyone, sending a smile in Levi's direction. His heart sped up as he took in the wraparound porch with hand-carved scrollwork in the corners of the posts.

Tall, grassy plants bordered the porch, purple flowers shooting up between the blades and thick stems.

Levi watched Rachel hug Hiram and Nettie while he lingered in the yard near the buggy. He listened to the pleasant exchange of words between family, wishing he'd had such a loving family. Levi had known of his dad's half-sister, but she'd warned Bruce to stay away because of his criminal nature. His dad's only brother, Eddie, had been dead since Levi was too little to remember him well. He'd missed out on having cousins and family the way most kids had. But here he was about to enter into a house where his cousin Abby was, and all he could see was Rachel.

As Hiram and Nettie slowly made their way inside the house, Rachel looked up, flashed another smile, and waved her hand for Levi to go inside with her.

"*Kume,* everyone is hungry."

Everyone?

Levi looked behind him at the line of buggies filling the yard. Why hadn't he seen them before? Her entire extended family must be here for the meal. How many were there? Would he be able to get lost in the mix, or would he stand out as the one who didn't belong? Was it too late to back out?

Rachel seemed to sense his hesitation. "You will fit in with us just fine. We are easy to get along with. Just be yourself."

That's the last thing I can be.

He was having a tough enough time walking in there as Levi Schrock, but he could never walk in there as Blake Monroe. They would *never* accept him. He was not like them. He didn't have the support of a family to build him up. He only had Bruce, who took every opportunity to tear him down to his level. It was best if these people never saw who Blake Monroe really was—especially Rachel.

Her smile could melt all the ugliness off him. All the lies, the petty crimes and the deceit. All of it washed away from his thoughts with one smile from her. In her presence, he felt the courage to be something better than he'd been his entire life. The man he was raised to be was not the man he wished to be. He wanted to be a man of honor—a man worthy of Rachel's love. But she did not know the real him, and if he could help it, she never would. If she did, she would surely turn her back on him.

Levi hesitated. "That's a lot of folks to meet all at once. I'm not sure I can go in there."

Rachel hooked her arm in his, sending shivers through him.

"*Mei familye* will be *gut* to you."

Levi swallowed a lump in his throat. "They already have. I don't deserve to be accepted like I'm a member of your family. I don't belong here."

He was practically blowing his cover, but his conscience would not allow him to deceive Hiram or Rachel anymore. In the week since he'd arrived, he'd felt more love and acceptance than he'd had his entire life. It was not something he'd earned, and he'd had a sudden revelation that maybe it was time to come clean with the truth.

CHAPTER 12

The screen door squeaked open and out came a woman who was slightly older than Rachel. She and Rachel had the same kind eyes, but there was something even more familiar in the way she looked. Levi thought she looked a little like *him*.

"There you are. *Mamm* is looking for you."

Rachel smiled at the woman. "Abby, this is Levi. He's the one I told you about. He's visiting from Ohio, near where you grew up."

So this was his cousin. No wonder she looked like him. Did either of them see the resemblance?

Levi managed a nervous smile. "It's nice to meet you."

Rachel turned to her sister. "I'll go see what *mamm* wants. Will you please convince Levi to go inside? He's nervous about being around everyone."

Abby sat in one of the rocking chairs on the porch and invited Levi to take the rocker next to hers.

"No one in there is going to bite you! Surely you're used to being around a lot of *familye.*"

"*N-nee.* My *d-daed* and I live in town and we don't see many others. We don't even have a buggy."

Levi tried to calm himself, hoping she wouldn't notice him stumbling over the Amish words.

"A big *familye* is nothing to be afraid of. In fact, sometimes there are so many of them you get lost and no one knows you're there unless you talk to them. Your *daed* is in Ohio alone?"

"*J-jah.* He hasn't been able to work for many years. He hurt his back. We've lived in town in a little rental house most of my life. I'll be sending most of my wages to him each week so he can pay the rent."

"Do you get help from the community?"

Levi thought about the things Bruce often *borrowed* from others in town. "*Jah,* sometimes."

Levi tried to change the subject. "Rachel tells me you lived in Barlow."

"*Jah.* Is that where you're from?"

"I live in Newport, along the Ohio River."

Abby wasn't sure what to think of him. "That's a long way to travel to look for work."

"I saw the advertisement in *The Budget.*"

Bruce had told him to look in the paper on the off-chance that there was a *Help Wanted* section, and to his surprise, this opportunity seemed to fall right into their laps.

Abby wasn't certain what it was about Levi, but she didn't trust him. "Normally *Englischers* answer those advertisements."

Levi smiled nervously. "The only *Englischer* I'm familiar with in those parts is Eddie Monroe."

Abby nearly choked on her own spit.

"He's famous in that area. There's claims that he buried a million dollars near the Ohio River. A lot of people have tried to find the money, but rumor has it he left a map to his only child."

Abby could feel the blood draining from her face. *She* was Eddie Monroe's only child—at least that's what she thought. But she didn't have any map leading her to a million dollars.

Levi hadn't missed the ashen look that crossed Abby's face at the mention of the map. Did she have it? Would she tell him even if she did?

"I've never heard such a tale. I lived there until I was ten years old and then again for a short time before I got married. I never once heard anything about that."

Levi smirked knowingly. "Maybe living in town has its advantages. You might not have heard it if you lived in the community away from the talk around town."

Abby shook her head. "*Nee,* I lived in town. I worked at *The Brick Oven* bakery. Surely I would have heard such a tale from one of the customers there. That's quite a wild notion. A million dollars is a lot of money. Why would the man have hidden the money instead of giving it to his daughter?"

Abby knew better than to open old wounds, but her curiosity was too strong to ignore.

Levi looked off in the distance somewhere in the yard, and focused on the line of family buggies that reminded him of why he was here. "They say he died just after he stole the money. And no one knows where his daughter is."

Abby gasped.

Eddie stole a million dollars and left her a map? Eddie's sister knew where she was. Her *aenti* had given her a book, *The Velveteen Rabbit,* that Eddie had with him the day he died. She'd received no map, and neither had her mother. The day he died they set in motion their plan to move back to the Amish community. Neither of them had attended Eddie's funeral. If anyone would know about the map, it would be his sister, wouldn't she? That is, if such a map even existed.

Abby giggled nervously. "That's quite a wild story you tell. Sorry I can't help you. I'd never heard such a wild tale before. I'd have remembered it if I'd heard something that outrageous."

Levi wondered why she was rambling. Did she know something? It was obvious by her tone and the way she fidgeted in her chair that she knew something. Would he get another chance to talk to her in order to gain her trust? Opportunities did not come along this easily. He figured he better take advantage of the fact she was talking and the conversation was already open to the subject. He needed information, and he needed it fast or he couldn't trust Bruce not to take matters into his own hands. He feared a visit from his dad. Bruce would force him to point out where Abby lived so he could search her house. He didn't trust the man not to hurt anyone that got in his way. The way he saw it, he had two choices. Press her for information and cause her to become suspicious; or he could let the matter drop and take his chances with Bruce.

CHAPTER 13

It was Rachel who made the decision for him when she poked her head out the screen door. "Are the two of you going to sit out here and gossip all night, or are you going to come in and join the *familye* for the meal?"

Her presence seemed to startle Abby, who hadn't said a word for several minutes. She stood up after shaking her head and walked into the house without saying a word.

Rachel turned to Levi. "What did you say to her? She seems a little rattled."

Levi wasn't sure if he should answer, but he knew she would probably find out anyway. Sisters confide in each other, don't they?

"I was telling her a story about a man and his stolen million dollars, and the map he left to his daughter. The guy is famous where I live. People are always caught digging around the Ohio River near my home and they get arrested for looking for the money. It's been hidden away almost as long as I've been alive, and not even the police can find it. Rumors have it that the money never existed, but that doesn't stop people from trying to find it."

Rachel leered at him. "Have *you* looked for the money?"

Levi wasn't expecting that question, and it caused his heart to thump.

"Of course not. I don't want that money, or anything it represents. It's stolen."

That part was now true. He knew how much that money had changed Bruce, and how bitter it had made him that his own brother had not told him where he hid the money before he died. That money was stolen and had been a source of pain throughout nearly his entire life. He no longer wanted anything to do with that money, even if it meant he would be poor his entire adulthood. He would not accept stolen money from Bruce, and he would never steal for him again. Since he'd been on the Miller farm, he'd learned the value of a hard day's work, and the wages he earned made him proud. Being here made him realize that he didn't need money or material possessions to be happy.

Rachel smiled and took his hand, leading him inside the house. Levi's heart did a somersault. Having her hand in his was all the confirmation he needed that it was time to turn his life around. Suddenly, he no longer cared about getting information out of Abby about the money. If he had anything to do with it, he would make sure Bruce would never lay eyes on that money. If he did manage to find the map, Bruce would have to get it without him.

Lord help me, I think I'm falling in love with Rachel.

ℬ𝒪ℛ

Dinner went better than Levi could have hoped for. Aside from a few odd looks from Hiram, Levi felt very comfortable with the extended family. They accepted him, and it felt good to be accepted for a change. He'd spent most of his life on the outside looking in at other families, and even envying them. But now, he almost felt like a part of this family. He listened to one story after another of good times they'd all shared, and he didn't feel left out even once. At the conclusion of the meal, the men went out into the barn while the women cleaned up the dishes. The men talked about their crops and horses and the proper style of suspender the Bishop had approved. Levi had never been happier to talk about so much *nothing* in all his life.

ℬ𝒪ℛ

When they returned to the Miller farm, Levi rushed to complete the evening chores so he could sneak out and meet up with Rachel. She had asked him if he would meet her at the end of the dock at the B&B, which was the halfway point between them. Levi knew from staying at the Schrock farm that the youth of the community would often sneak out late at night to meet with a potential crush. He was certainly hoping that Rachel's invitation meant she was interested in him. If not, he still intended to enjoy her company.

The crickets disguised his footfalls as he neared the dock where Rachel was waiting for him. The warm summer breeze ruffled little wisps of her hair that had come out of her *kapp*. He walked slowly to the end of the dock, not wanting to disturb her. His hands felt sweaty, and he mentally reminded himself to stay calm. He'd never really had time to consider dating before, especially since he had to drop out of school to take care of Bruce.

Rachel turned around, her face looking lovely with the pale moonlight shimmering against her dainty features. Levi didn't think he had ever seen a more lovely young woman than Rachel. She smiled briefly and invited him to sit next to her on the end of the dock.

Rachel let her bare feet swish and splash in the pond water. "You can take your shoes off and join me if you'd like."

Levi hoped his feet smelled okay as he started to remove his boots. Just in case, he plunked his bare feet into the water just as soon as the socks came off.

"Ahhh. The cool water feels good on such a warm night."

"Whatever you said to *mei schweschder,* Abby, really upset her. She pulled me aside after dinner and told me to stay away from you."

Levi's heart felt like it skipped a beat or two. "I didn't mean to upset her. I was just making conversation. I guess I should know better than to repeat gossip. Tell her I'm sorry."

Levi seriously regretted every word. Talk like that could blow his cover. But what did he really need his disguise for anymore? Would Hiram keep him on as a farm hand the way the Schrock's had? Probably not once he learned of Levi's deceit. What could he do? There was no taking it back now. He worried he would probably be asked to leave, and that was the last thing he wanted.

Rachel nudged him with her elbow and smiled.

"I'll tell her. But for the record, I have no intention of taking her advice where you're concerned."

Levi smiled. He would have never thought that sitting on the end of a dock with his feet dangling in the water and staring at a pretty girl could make him feel so happy.

CHAPTER 14

Rachel tossed about trying to sleep, but all she could do was think of Levi. She would have to be up in just a few short hours to open the bakery, but none of that mattered at the moment. She'd had to sneak into the *haus* after spending a little too much time out on the dock talking with Levi. She was certain that Rose and Noah had seen them out on the dock from across the pond at his *haus,* but she knew her friend would keep her secret.

As the night wore on, she'd hoped Levi might try to kiss her at the conclusion of their time together, but much to her disappointment, he hadn't.

From the way he'd spoken, she'd gathered he and his *daed* had not spent much time if any at all in their own community. She didn't blame him for the lack of knowledge about farming. From what she understood, the only time he'd spent on a farm and doing chores had been sparse visits with his cousin. He'd even admitted to her that the only times he'd gone to Sunday services at the church was with his cousin the previous summer. He'd confided in her that it had sparked an interest in knowing *Gott* more closely.

Rachel rolled over and stared out her window at the moon. It had seemed almost magical sitting under the moonlight with Levi. The thought of it made her giddy. Was it possible that she was falling in *lieb* with Levi? Certainly Abby would scold her for thinking such things. After all, she barely knew him. What she had learned about him as they'd conversed on the dock late last night had made her feel a lot of compassion for him. It seemed he'd led a pretty sheltered life away from the community and more among the *Englisch*. He seemed more worldly than most Amish *buwes* her age, but it attracted her to him even more than she was willing to admit to herself. She'd considered spending time among the *Englisch* the way her *schweschder* and her *mamm* had at her same age, but maybe now she wouldn't have to. With Levi there, it seemed the *Englisch* had come directly to her through *him*.

ଞ୦ଘ

Levi couldn't sleep even though he would have to be up in a few hours to milk the cows and do the morning chores which would begin his busy day. His mind wandered to Rachel. It seemed he couldn't keep his mind off her since he'd met her that very first time when he'd come into the bakery with Bruce. It had been Bruce's idea to check out the community and the surrounding area. He said he needed to know where everything was—just in case. In case of what, Levi had no idea, and he wasn't sure he even wanted to know. But he'd hoped it was for reasons of helping him to get to know everyone he needed to get information from.

Now that he had met most of Rachel's family, he felt worse about the deception and what he was doing. If he told Rachel the truth, would she forgive him for lying to her? He needed the work, and if her grandfather found out about his deception, he could be fired. Then he would have no choice but to return to a life of crime with Bruce. How could he be honest with her and still protect his own interests?

Lord, help me to be honest. Help me to give up my selfish ways and think of other's needs instead of my own.

A peaceful calm warmed him to his very core. Was that God telling him it would work out if he told her the truth? He *had* to tell her. His conscience was eating away at him. She'd asked him to meet her again the following night at the dock and he would have to find a way to tell her then. In the meantime, would he be able to tell Hiram? Admittedly, he was afraid of losing his job, but not having the respect of his employer would feel worse to him.

The light on his cell phone blinked. Why was Bruce messaging him at this late hour? Levi scrolled through the twenty-plus messages that ranged from *"I want an update."* to *"Where are you?"*, and everything in-between. The newest was a demand to answer him immediately.

Levi sent a return text asking him what the problem was. He was sure he already knew. Bruce was more than likely drunk and had decided to do some thinking before he passed out. The phone lit up indicating Bruce had answered.

Levi read the text message. *"I want my money NOW!"*

What could he say to defuse his drunken father, and calm him enough to keep him from coming into the community and causing trouble? Could he tell him that he spoke to Abby? Bruce was not that dumb—even when heavily intoxicated. He would want a solid answer and to know that progress was being made to locate the money he intended to claim as his own. Bruce had taught him to lie. Should he use that against the man, and lie to him now? Levi told himself that it was only to protect Rachel and her family, but even that would not make it right.

Lord, please forgive me for lying to this man who is my earthly father, but I can't let him hurt the people I have grown to love.

Before he lost his nerve, Levi's fingers began to roll over the keys to form a message to Bruce. He hoped it would be enough to stave him off while giving him the illusion that he had a handle on the situation. He pushed *send* on his final text. *"I am very close to getting to the truth."*

CHAPTER 15

After a fairly sleepless night, Levi rose from the bed reluctantly so he could begin his day. The sun was just making its way over the edge of the horizon, boasting beautiful crimson, amber, and violet highlights across the sparse clouds gathered there. Chickens rallied in the yard for their feed, the roosters crowing relentlessly.

I thought you were only supposed to crow once when the sun came up? You haven't shut up for the past twenty minutes!

Hiram hadn't yet made it to the barn, and Levi was content with the animals to keep him company. With Hiram here, he might be tempted to spill his guts about why he was here. The light of day had changed his mind about such foolish thoughts. He was prepared to continue the charade in order to keep the weekly wages flowing to Bruce. At least until he could think of a way out of this mess.

Once he reached the fields, he would be out there alone for the entire day. Hiram, according to Nettie, was still too tired to work in the hot sun. Although he felt bad for his boss, he was determined to keep clear from him as much as possible and do a thorough job to really earn his wages. Being only his second week at the Miller's, he was determined to prove his worth and keep his job—even if that meant lying to his own father. Meeting this family had already taught him the value of others. His loyalties were beginning to take root in this family, and he would not let them down.

The breeze rustled the corn stalks that had grown tall enough that Levi could barely see over the tops of them. This was the life he desired; there was no doubt about it. The hard work didn't bother him. He suddenly found joy in working for his meals. How would he be able to provide for himself once this job ended? He had to start thinking of his future. He didn't want to end up like Bruce. He hated the thought of leaving, but he couldn't go on deceiving the people of the community. Was it possible for him to convert? Did the Amish even allow such a thing?

The clanging of the Miller's dinner bell rang in Levi's ears. He looked up at the sun that was still low in the eastern sky. It wasn't close enough to noon for him to return for a meal. His heart pounded in his chest. Something was wrong! Levi took off running toward the house, not thinking of anything but his friends and their well-being.

When he cleared the rows of corn, all he could see was Nettie crouched on the ground near the back porch. She was hovering over Hiram, who lay lifeless in the dirt.

Levi skidded to a stop just short of them and collapsed next to his boss. "What happened? Did he have another spell?"

Nettie's face was flush and she didn't take her eyes off her husband. "I don't know. I found him out here when I came out to empty the mop-bucket."

Levi was relieved when he could see that Hiram was still breathing. "Did you call the doctor?"

Nettie shook her head. "I don't know how to use the phone in the barn."

Levi scrambled to his feet and ran to the barn. It was the second time in a week that he would make the call for his boss and friend.

After hanging up with Dr. Davis, Levi ran out to tell Nettie he was on his way. The relief in her eyes put a lump in his throat.

"Let's get him inside and see if we can get him to drink some water."

Nettie nodded, not looking up from her husband, whose head was nestled in her lap. He seemed to go in and out of consciousness, and that worried Levi. Putting a hand under Hiram's arm, he and Nettie helped the man inside the house like they had the previous week. Was this going to be a regular thing? Levi hoped not.

"Help me upstairs," Hiram mumbled.

Levi was happy to hear him speaking coherently, even if he didn't seem to have any strength whatsoever. Wrapping Hiram's arm around his shoulder, Levi hung onto his wrist for leverage, and put his other arm around the man's torso to keep him snug at his side for the trip up the stairs. Nettie stayed behind her husband to help steady him, making the short journey a little more manageable. Once inside the small room, Levi steered his boss toward the bed. He pivoted the man with one quick movement, putting him square in the middle of the bed. Nettie rushed to his head, resting it gently on his pillow and smoothing back his hair.

"He feels a little warm like he did last time. I'll get a cool cloth for his forehead."

Levi went to the window and pushed it open to bring in the breeze that had kept him cool out in the field all morning. Storm clouds were rolling in, and Levi was grateful. They could use some rain.

Since when do I care if it rains?

He looked over at his boss lying helplessly on his bed.

I care because this man has been so good to me. Lord, bring the rain for this man's vegetables that he grows to feed his family. Please bring healing to Hiram. He's an honorable man, and I can't bear to lose him.

Levi turned from the window, but looked back out toward the road when he heard the thunderous footfalls of a horse being pushed to its limits to get the doctor here quickly. Nettie rushed back into the room with a wet cloth and a glass of water for her husband.

Levi tipped his hat. "I'm going out to take care of the doc's horse. I'll be back when the he's had a chance to examine Hiram."

Nettie looked up briefly, sending a smile of thanks to him. Levi walked out of the room feeling he didn't deserve her trust.

CHAPTER 16

"Do you want me to take you home?" Levi asked. "It won't take long to hitch up the pony cart."

Rachel sighed. "I'd rather walk. Will you walk with me?"

Levi nodded. The rest of the family had left Hiram's home an hour before, but Rachel had stayed behind to wash dishes and straighten the kitchen for Nettie so she could remain at her husband's side.

During his exam, it had come out that Hiram had been suffering for more than a year with a heart condition that the doctor had under control with medication. But now, it seemed his current dose was failing him. Doctor Davis had some concern that Hiram had suffered a mild heart attack, but the stubborn man would not agree to a trip to the hospital. After an increase in his medication, he was already starting to regain his coloring. That didn't stop Levi from worrying about him.

After walking some distance in total silence except for the occasional crunch of a rock under foot, Rachel nudged Levi. "Why are you so quiet tonight? Last night I could barely get in a single word. Now, I think I could talk for an hour, and I fear you might not hear a word of it."

"I'm worried. I know I shouldn't be, but I can't help it."

Rachel cupped her arm in Levi's, sending a wave of heat coursing through him.

"I always find that if I'm worried about something, distraction always works."

She was right. He was currently so distracted by her arm being intertwined with his, he could barely think of anything else. It was comforting to have her so near him, and that was a feeling he didn't think he could ever live without. In the short time since he'd come to work for Hiram, he'd never felt more accepted than he did right now. Was it possible she would still like him even if she knew the truth? The Amish seemed to give their love unconditionally, and that confused him. He'd always had to earn any attention, good or bad, from Bruce. It usually came with a price.

The cricket's song filled the warm summer air, while the gentle breeze rustled the leaves on the trees that lined the road. This was the most peaceful Levi had felt his entire life. How could he give this up? How could he give up Rachel when his job here was done? The truth was; he didn't think he could, even if he wanted to.

"Do you allow outsiders into your community?"

Rachel looked at him briefly. "You mean *Englischers?*"

"*Jah.*"

She smiled warmly. "We have had a few *Englischers,* and even a few from other communities join us. Our Bishop is very lenient. Isn't yours?"

Levi cleared his throat. "I don't know that much about him. I only met him a few times when I attended services with my cousin. My *daed* isn't exactly a church-going man."

Rachel tightened her grip on his arm. "How sad for you. Has your *daed* turned his back on the church?"

Levi shrugged. "Somehow I doubt he was ever a believer. But I am. I'm very new to my faith, though."

Rachel kicked at rocks along the road. "I can't imagine my life without my faith."

Levi swallowed hard. "I feel the same way. I don't know how I managed my entire life without it."

Rachel giggled. It was one of the most pleasant sounds Levi had ever heard. He couldn't remember the last time he *really* laughed.

"Now that you have it, you will never be without it. *Gott* is never far from us unless we turn our backs on Him. What about your *mamm?*"

That wasn't a question Levi cared to address. How could he tell her his mother had been a prostitute and that his father had been her regular companion? The way his dad told the story, his mother had dropped him off on Bruce's doorstep two days after he'd been born, and then went back to her profession.

She'd visited sparsely until he was about seven years old, but he didn't remember her—not that he cared to.

"I don't know where she is. According to my *daed,* she dropped me off after I was born and only saw me a handful of times. I don't know her."

Rachel slowed her steps as they neared her farm. "Perhaps that was the turning point for your *daed* that made him turn his back on *Gott.* Maybe it hurt him too deeply to trust anymore. Grief will make a person question everything."

Was Rachel correct? Had his father loved his mother so much that it changed him when she chose to return to a life of prostitution over staying with him and raising their child? Was it possible Bruce was a better man before she left him? Probably not if he was frequently visiting with a prostitute. Still, it made him wonder why Bruce had made the choice to care for him instead of getting rid of him like his own mother had. Why had he raised him so harshly? Was it possible his father blamed him for his mother leaving?

"I suppose anything is possible. He is a bitter man. Has been as long as I can remember."

Rachel let her arm slip until her fingers met his. She slowly intertwined her fingers in his, sending tingling jitters through him.

"I'm so sorry you missed out on having your *mamm* raise you."

Levi turned to face her. "Nettie is so kind to me; she makes me wonder what it would have been like to grow up with two parents instead of one."

"She has been very *gut* for *mei grossdaddi.* That's how I know he will fight his weakness—to stay with her. They haven't been together very long, and I know he is not yet ready to leave her."

Levi pushed down the lump in his throat. Where had all this emotion suddenly come from? If Bruce would ever catch him as close to tears as he was now, he'd take a switch to him. His dad had always told him that crying made him look weak. Right now, he felt pretty weak, but he welcomed the strength God seemed to be offering him at the moment.

CHAPTER 17

The rest of the week was very busy for Levi as he took over the entire workload of Hiram's farm by himself. Hiram's sons and grandsons had all offered to help, but he told them he had complete confidence in his hired hand. That confidence filled Levi with the courage to face every new experience with enthusiasm. With only a few verbal instructions, Levi felt ready for each day. He was so busy, he'd neglected his contact with Bruce. He had saved his only free time to be spent with Rachel. He knew he couldn't ignore Bruce indefinitely, but he wished he could.

As he shuffled in from the fields alone for the third day in a row, Levi felt both exhaustion and exhilaration at having completed an honest day's work. His clothing was dusty, and he felt like he had ten pounds of dirt on his skin. He lifted the straw hat from his head and fanned the back of his neck. Aside from keeping the sun off his face, he couldn't see what purpose the hat served. It made him too warm, but he wore it to prevent even more suspicion against him than he already felt. He didn't dare speak much to Nettie when she served him lunch, for fear he might say the wrong thing. When Hiram instructed him, he listened intently and didn't do much more than nod his answers.

He needed a shower, but he didn't want to go into the house just yet. He'd eyed the pond at the far end of the property several times, thinking it looked like a refreshing spot to take a dip. Walking toward the water, he could feel the temperature in the breeze shifting a few degrees cooler. Already he felt refreshed, but the anticipation of the cool water was too much temptation to resist as he began to unbutton his shirt. Pushing down his suspenders, he let them fall to his sides as he loosened the shirttails from his trousers. Pulling off his boots and socks brought even more relief.

Levi stepped toward the edge of the pond where frogs sunned themselves lazily on top of water-lily leaves. The water was clear in the bright sunlight, the dark, sandy bottom inviting his toes to burrow in the cool mud. From the house, he could hear the faint clang of the dinner bell, but he was too preoccupied with taking a quick swim to rinse off the dust and sweat of a hard day's work.

The moment his feet sank in the muddy bottom, dirt clouds swirled around his feet. He didn't care; the water brought instant relief to his overheated body. With the bottoms of his pant-legs now submerged, he wondered if it would be more practical to continue or remove the pants and swim in his boxers. Knowing how conservative the Amish were, he decided it was best to leave the pants on in case anyone should spot him swimming. With Hiram's sister, Bess, running the B&B that bordered the pond, he knew it was possible she could have guests that would be out on the water using the canoes or paddle-boats she rented out.

Wading out a little further past the lilies and croaking frogs, Levi dove under and swam a good stretch in the sparkling water. To him, this was better than taking a shower, and much more refreshing. As his head broke the surface of the still water, he could see Rachel standing on the shore looking out at him. While treading water, he watched as she pulled of her shoes and stockings and stepped into the edge of the water.

She cupped her hand over her mouth and shouted out to him. "Are you going to come in and eat dinner? I rang the bell, but when you didn't come in, Nettie sent me to look for you."

He swam toward her, making ripples on the smooth surface of the water. When he reached shallow water, he stood, exposing his bare chest. He wasn't shy about his looks; he had always worked out and took pride in his six-pack abs. But the look of shock on Rachel's face told him he should hurry to the shore and put his shirt on. The strange thing was, she didn't look away even though he expected her to. Was it possible she was attracted to his physical side?

He stood in front of her, allowing her to look at him. Was it wrong that he wanted to pull her into his arms and kiss her? From the look on her face, he would guess she was thinking the same thing.

She blinked. "I brought left-over bread from the bakery—for dinner."

Rachel chided herself for blurting out such a random statement. But she couldn't take her eyes off Levi's muscular frame, and she had no idea what to do about it. His wet hair lay to one side, and his water-soaked pants clung to him. His bare chest glistening against the low-lying sun. If she wasn't so worried about him thinking ill of her, she would have kissed him right there. The temptation to reach out and touch his bare flesh surprised her.

She stumbled backward. "Do you want me to get you a towel so you can dry off before you come in for dinner?"

Levi smiled at her. He could see how much his presence made her nervous, and he found it cute. If he kissed her would she run off? Or would she let him?

Levi shook the inappropriate thoughts from his mind. "A towel would be very nice. *Danki.*"

CHAPTER 18

Levi rode into town, grateful the horse knew where she was going because he couldn't concentrate on the road at all. His thoughts were too preoccupied to notice the *Englischers* bustling around conducting business with the many Amish shops in town. He didn't even feel particularly nervous about his weekly visit with Bruce. He almost felt invincible as he steered the horse along the outskirts of town to the little motel in which Bruce had taken up residence.

His mind kept drifting to the night before and the look on Rachel's face when he'd stepped out of the pond shirtless and dripping wet. He reveled in the way she'd looked at him with a yearning in her eyes. They'd continued to eye one another throughout dinner, and when he walked her home, she'd let him hold her hand. He could almost feel the warmth of her hand even now.

As Levi stepped down from the pony cart, he felt a tight grip on the back of his collar catching him off guard.

"Boy, what took you so long?" Bruce dragged him by the arm into his motel room.

Levi nearly gagged from the smell. The drapes were pulled closed, but he could see the sheets on the double bed were stained with vomit. An old rotary-dial phone sat on the single night stand beside a digital clock radio. The numbers on the clock flipped to the hour and the radio blared out an oldies tune. Bruce lurched toward it and slammed the snooze button on the top.

"I don't know how to shut that thing off. I tried to set the alarm, but I can't get it to stop playing that loud music. I didn't want to unplug it because I need to know what time it is."

Levi could see that Bruce was hung-over and not thinking straight because of it, so he went over to the clock and adjusted the off button. "It should stay off now. You just push this button right here."

Levi didn't know why he was bothering to explain it to his father. He would only get drunk again and forget what he said. He stepped toward the doorway for some fresh air as he reached into his pocket and pulled out his weekly wages. As expected, Bruce snatched the money from his fingers and counted out the bills.

Bruce snarled. "I don't think that Amish farmer is paying you enough. You look tired from all the work. And this ain't enough for me to live on." He waved the bills at him.

Levi walked out the door, and then turned to face his father. "Then I suggest you get your own job." Levi tossed the cell phone at Bruce. "And stop calling me and texting me. You take the phone. I don't want it, and I won't hide it anymore. I'll see you next Saturday."

Levi hopped in the pony cart and clicked to the horse. He knew it wasn't right the way he spoke to Bruce, but he didn't feel there was any other way to communicate with him.

"What about my money?" Bruce called after him.

"I'm working on it," Levi hollered as he pushed the horse to a fast trot.

The real Levi Schrock had told him over the past summer that he was to honor his mother and his father. How could he honor a mother who left him and a father who abused him? Bruce didn't understand his son's kindness—he never had. Maybe it was time for a little tough love.

ಬೂಞ

Rachel turned over the sign on the bakery door to let her customers know it was open for the day. She'd spent most of the morning making flower-shaped cookies and daydreaming about Levi. As she frosted the last batch of cookies with the variety of pastel-colored frosting, she heard the jingling of the bell on the front door. She poked her head around the side of the kitchen, surprised to see Levi entering the bakery. Her heart fluttered until she caught the expression on his face. He looked distraught; perhaps he'd received bad news from back home. She hoped whatever it was wouldn't lead him away from the community so soon. Not when she had only begun to get to know him.

She came around the side of the kitchen, towel in hand, as she tried to wipe frosting from her fingertips. "*Gudemariye,* Levi. What brings you here?"

He looked at her cheerful face and her beautiful, smiling green eyes. That was all he needed to bring his spirit up.

"I missed my breakfast this morning since I drove into town early. I was hoping you might have some fresh biscuits and honey. I'm starving."

Rachel giggled. "I hardly think you're starving, but I'd be happy to get you something. Would you like *kaffi?*"

"*Jah, danki.*" Levi felt awkward using the words he'd learned from the Schrock's, but he already felt like his world was falling apart. He didn't need to add losing Rachel too. He had to keep her suspicion of him to a minimum.

Rachel motioned for him to sit at one of the small tables along the windows while she went into the kitchen to get the items for a small breakfast for Levi. As she poured his *kaffi,* she wondered what it would be like to serve him breakfast every morning as his *fraa* someday. Her cheeks heated. She tried to look down, but Levi had already noticed.

He smiled. "I could get used to this."

His comment took her by surprise, causing her cheeks to burn with embarrassment. He took her hand in his and gave it a squeeze. A shy giggle escaped her lips, but she quickly straightened and leveled her expression.

Rachel cleared her throat. "I don't have any biscuits, but I have banana nut muffins. Would you like one?"

Levi shook his head while he sipped the hot beverage. He let her hand slip from his grasp, but she allowed it to linger there. He cupped his fingers around hers again and asked her to sit with him. At her touch, his worries suddenly seemed to slip away.

CHAPTER 19

Levi felt funny sitting on the backless wooden bench during church services. It was his first one in this community, but not his first ever. Hiram had insisted Levi and Nettie bring him to the Yoder home for service, despite the doctor's orders for him to remain in bed for another few days. Hiram had stated his case to the two of them, saying that he would take it easy after they went back home.

Levi would never forget the day that the Schrock's had hosted the service in their home while he was staying with them. It had intrigued him, and given him a hunger for God's word. He'd sat on the stairs and looked over the service, witnessing how God had brought the families and friends together, and he had craved that unconditional love the Amish shared with their community.

Now, as Levi sat among them, he felt as though he was betraying their trust. They had taken him at his word that he was who he said he was. Would his word mean nothing to them if they found out his true identity? He had been welcomed with open arms with no questions asked. Did he deserve their trust? Did he deserve *Rachel's* trust? How would she react if she knew the truth? Would she reject his feelings for her?

Levi glanced over at Rachel, who was sitting across the set of benches from him. She locked eyes with Levi, fluttering her long, auburn lashes in a flirtatious manner. He enjoyed the attention, sending her a smile of appreciation. His heart yearned to belong here, but who was he kidding? Being deceitful was not from God.

Lord, help me to find a way to tell these people who I really am. Help me to have the courage to be myself, even if they turn their backs on me.

ဆဝၺ

Rachel couldn't keep her attention on the service. Thankfully, Katie, Rose, and Abby all faced forward, and had no idea what Rachel was up to. If they had, she would surely have gotten a scolding from each of them—even though they had done the same thing when they had new love interests. Rachel, however, wanted to keep her relationship with Levi a secret since he lived with her *grossdaddi.* Keeping her relationship a secret the way all the youth did made her feel very grown up. Since her sixteenth birthday a few weeks ago, she'd felt no difference, but the possibility of having a beau made all the difference in the world.

Rachel fidgeted in her seat, determined to face forward and pay attention to the service. She could see out of the corner of her eye every time Levi stole a glance in her direction, and it caused her to smile. Did he like her as much as she liked him? Since she'd turned sixteen, she'd been invited to youth singings by two of the local young *menner,* but those dates never amounted to anything. Levi was a different story. They hadn't attended any of the usual youth gatherings, yet they had already developed a deep friendship in such a short time.

At the conclusion of the service, Rachel signaled Levi with her eyes so he would follow her. She ran out of the *haus* before her *mamm* could ask her to help with the meal. Her *mamm* had Abby and the others to help. The kitchen was always too crowded anyway, and Rachel doubted she would be missed. She entered the barn and retreated to the loft, where she often went to think. Sometimes she would sit at the pond, but she was usually spotted by someone. Today, she wanted seclusion.

Levi climbed the ladder to the loft and sat beside her, his feet dangling over the edge. "So this is where you live?"

"*Jah,* it was our turn to host services. I'm supposed to be inside "hosting", but my *familye* can handle it. Was our service the same as in your community?"

"I've only been a few times with my cousin, but it seemed like it was the same."

Levi pulled her hand into his. "Will you have time to meet me at the dock tonight? Hiram is getting better, so Nettie won't need me after I finish the evening chores."

Rachel smiled. "I will need to help Abby and *mamm* after everyone leaves, but I'm certain I will be done in time. Should we meet at dusk?"

Levi pulled her hand to his lips and kissed the back of it. "Sounds like a plan. Should we get back before someone comes looking for us?"

Rachel stared at him. "Can't we stay here until everyone leaves? I'm not up for visiting today."

Levi rubbed her hand across his whiskery chin and then kissed it again. "I would love to stay here all day with you, but I don't want to get you into trouble."

Rachel smiled. "If I didn't know better, I'd think that's exactly what you wanted to do."

Smiling, Levi kissed her hand once again.

"Maybe, but we are young. We have our whole lives ahead of us. Let's go hang out with the old people. It's their time now."

Rachel wasn't sure what he meant by that, but she had an idea he was talking about her *grossdaddi's* health. She hadn't allowed herself to think about it much for fear that she would have to face life without him. She was not ready for that. She had made light of his poor health for a while, unwilling to think about him as old and most likely nearing his end.

Rachel tightened her grip on Levi's hand. "I suppose you're right. We will have plenty of time to talk at the dock later on."

"And I can do this." Levi kissed her hand again.

Having Levi so near gave Rachel a sense of security she liked. She could be herself with him, and he understood her without much explanation. That was something she could see in her future, and it was enough encouragement to join the others—for now.

CHAPTER 20

After the shared meal following church services, Rachel was eager to get the dishes done so she could meet Levi at the dock. She hoped her *aenti* Bess, who'd left an hour ago would be asleep by the time she and Levi met. Her *aenti* had complained of a stomach ache before her husband, Jessup took her home. She claimed she intended to go to bed early, and Rachel hoped she would. Tomorrow being wash day, most of the women in the community went to bed early on Sunday evenings, but it was barely dusk and Rachel hoped the woman would be fast asleep by the time she reached the dock, especially since there weren't currently any guests staying at the B&B.

"Why are you in such a hurry tonight? I've never seen you wash dishes so fast," Abby said.

Rachel didn't stop to look at her *schweschder.*

"I was thinking of all I have to do tomorrow. We have a lot of wash to do before I have to go to the bakery to start Tuesday's baking."

Abby snickered. "It's going to be an even longer day if you stay out too late with Levi tonight."

Rachel felt her heart slam against her ribcage.

"Levi and I are just friends."

"Any time someone says they are *just* friends with someone it means they are more than *just* friends."

Rachel pursed her lips. "That's not always true. We are *just* friends."

Abby struggled to wipe the dishes as fast as Rachel washed them. "That's how it started with me and Jonah."

Rachel broke her momentum long enough to stare her *schweschder* down. "That's different. You and Jonah grew up together. Me and Levi only just met a few weeks ago."

Abby put the dishtowel down. "I see the way the two of you look at each other, and the way your eyes light up when he's near."

Rachel narrowed her eyes. "Alright, I'll admit I like him. But please don't tell. Can we just keep it a secret between us?"

Abby hugged her younger *schweschder.* "No one knows more than I do how important it is to keep a relationship quiet. Rumors and gossip nearly kept me and Jonah apart. I will keep your secret, if you will keep mine."

Rachel's eyes widened. "What secret?"

Abby smiled. "Jonah and I are expecting a *boppli.*"

Rachel squealed.

Abby shushed her.

"Go and meet Levi, I'll finish up these dishes."

Rachel squealed again and hugged Abby.

"*Danki.* I'm happy for you and Jonah."

Abby smiled. "I know you are. Now go, before I change my mind."

"Why are you keeping the news a secret? *Mamm* and *daed* would be so happy to hear they are going to have *grandkinner.*"

"We wanted to wait until the end of harvest to tell everyone so the *familye* won't stop everything they're doing to make quilts and furniture and clothes. You understand what big news this is."

"*Jah.* You're right. *Mamm* won't get any canning done because she will be too eager to start sewing. *Onkel* Seth will insist on making a cradle and rocking chair instead of helping with the harvest. I see what you mean. I will be happy to keep your secret, but even after you tell everyone, you still have to keep mine."

Abby smiled. "Of course I will."

Rachel wiped her hands on the dishtowel and kissed Abby on the cheek. "*Danki.* See you later."

Rachel ran upstairs to put on a clean dress and comb out her waist-length hair. The sun had lightened her auburn hair to a dark blond, and she really liked the lighter color. She was tempted to leave her hair down, but wasn't sure she should risk getting caught with her *kapp* off. She knew that other girls in the community had done such a thing in private with their beaus, but she was still unsure of Levi or the rules of his community—or if he even belonged to one.

Rachel crept down the stairs quietly, being careful to avoid the squeaky step. The sitting room was devoid of all *familye,* so she slipped out the front door, closing it quietly behind her. Once outside on the porch, she breathed a little easier. How did her friends manage to sneak out every night to meet their beaus? She figured they must have gotten pretty *gut* at it since she hadn't seen any of them except at Sunday services all summer.

ಐಲಿ

Levi's palms became sweaty as he paced the length of the dock over and again. What was he thinking getting involved with Rachel while he was there to do a job and get out of the community? The last thing he wanted to do was hurt her, and if she learned why he was really there, it might ruin things between them. He wondered if he should just do his job, get on with his life, and leave her behind where she would always be safe, or if he should take his chances and tell her the truth.

Either way, she's going to get hurt. So why not stick it out and try to help her through it—if she'll let me.

Rachel stepped onto the dock with bare feet. The smell of honeysuckle filled the humid air, and the crickets quieted their song at her presence. Fireflies hovered around the large oak tree beside the dock, and an occasional mosquito buzzed her ear. She must have missed that spot with *Mamm's* herbal repellant. She'd been in too big a hurry to get out of the *haus* before she was caught to worry about getting every prime spot that the annoying bugs like to attack. Now she wished she'd taken the time to douse every inch. She hated the thought of swatting at bugs while trying to have what she hoped would be a romantic evening.

Levi approached her. "Mosquitoes bothering you?"

Rachel sighed. *"Jah.* I neglected to put *Mamm's* herbal repellant everywhere. I was in a hurry and must have missed a few spots."

Levi chuckled. "I may have a little too much on. Come here and I will hide you from them for a minute until they get the hint and fly away."

Rachel wasn't sure what his meaning was, but she stepped closer to him anyway. Suddenly, he scooped her up in his arms and buried his face in the crook of her neck. Instinctively, she wrapped her arms around his waist. It was nice being in his arms. She felt safe and *loved.*

Levi sucked in a deep breath. "You smell very nice."

"That's *Mamm's* herbs from her garden." With her face buried in his chest, her words came out muffled.

Levi snuggled her closer. "I don't smell any herbs; I think it's just the way you smell. It's beautiful—like you."

Rachel's heart fluttered. Was she falling in love with Levi already?

CHAPTER 21

There was no telling how long Levi had held Rachel in his arms before a sudden splash in the water broke the spell between them. Levi looked out toward the water in time to see a family of ducks swimming into the center of the pond.

Rachel giggled. "That scared me. I thought there was someone out here."

Levi took her hand and led her to the end of the dock. "Maybe we shouldn't stand here like this in case someone does come along. I wouldn't want anyone to misunderstand."

Rachel allowed him to steer her like a horse to the end of the dock, where they sat down, letting their feet dangle in the water. What had he meant by his statement? Had she been the only one enjoying their embrace?

Once they were settled, Levi lifted her hand in his and pressed the back of it to his lips. "Don't get me wrong; I would love to stand there and hold you for the rest of the night, but I wouldn't want to get you into any trouble."

Rachel nudged him with her hip. "We're in our *rumspringa,* Levi; we won't be accountable until we are baptized."

Levi cleared his throat. "I-uh-I know that."

"Has it been hard for you not being part of the community while you were growing up?"

How could he answer her without giving himself away for the fraud he was?

"I don't know as much as I should about the rules of the ordnung. I only know what my cousin has told me while I visited him."

Rachel looked at him. "That might explain a few things."

Levi raised an eyebrow. "Such as?"

Rachel's eyes softened. "Why you stumble over your words, and why you don't know how to do some things that most of us as Amish take for granted."

Levi nodded agreement.

Rachel rested her head on his shoulder. "Your *mamm*...she was an *Englischer?"*

"Jah."

It wasn't exactly a lie. Just because he and Bruce were *Englischers* too, didn't mean he wasn't telling her the truth.

"That might explain why she didn't stay with you. She might not have wanted to adhere to the ordnung. Many *Englischers* can't. They say they want to at first, but they find it is too difficult to give up the modern conveniences of the world."

Levi thought he could give up everything except air and food to be with Rachel. He wanted no part of the world he'd been raised in or the harshness that came with it.

"I've thought about it most of my life and I can't make any sense of it. If there's anything I can take from my childhood, it would be to do the exact opposite with my children than the way I was brought up. My children will never have to wonder if I love them."

Rachel felt heat rise in her cheeks. "Abby says the same thing sometimes. I wonder if it's because her biological father abandoned her. She doesn't talk about it much, but when I was younger, I would hear her praying about it."

Levi kicked at the water, his legs swinging over the edge of the dock. "I can't imagine not wanting to watch my child grow up. What kind of a person abandons their own child?"

"Sometimes it's what is best for the child. My *onkel* and *aenti* adopted a little girl because the birth mother couldn't raise her on her own. I think, in that case, she did a very *gut* thing for her daughter. But then there are times when a parent acts selfishly, as in my *schweschder's* case, and maybe yours too. But even though Abby's *daed* was selfish for leaving her, it was still what was best for her. Do you think that could be the case for you too?"

Levi sighed, swallowing the lump in his throat.

"I honestly think I would have been better off if they *both* would have abandoned me. Neither of them was prepared to be the kind of parent a child needs."

"Is your *daed* harsh with you?" Rachel wasn't sure if she should pry, but it seemed Levi wanted to confide in her. She admired his openness and honesty about his life, and she felt honored that he would trust *her* with his most private thoughts.

Levi wasn't sure if he should open that can of worms or not. He wanted to tell her everything about his life—to tell her the truth about why he was here, but something still held him back. Was it fear? If he had to be honest with himself, he would say he feared rejection from her. The Amish had been the only people to ever love and care for him the way he needed. Now, Rachel was one of the few really good relationships in his life, and he didn't want to risk losing her.

"He has always been harsh for as long as I can remember. He hasn't been a good example, or even a good person."

Rachel allowed herself to snuggle closer to Levi, and he put his arm around her.

"I'm sorry you have to live with that. But you will be old enough to be on your own soon. Have you given any thought to what your future holds?"

He gave her shoulder a squeeze. "I do every day."

CHAPTER 22

Levi couldn't concentrate on poor Lulu's milking. He'd almost told Rachel the truth about himself the night before. What a relief that would have been. But he also knew that now was not the time to reveal his true identity. He needed to keep it a secret just a little longer until he could go to Bruce at the end of the week and tell him he was out of the deal he'd made with him. Rachel had encouraged him to separate himself from his dad and to stand on his own. He would be eighteen soon, and that meant he needed to stand up for himself and become a man—the man *he* wanted to be instead of the man Bruce had taught him to be.

Levi patted the Holstein cow on her side, apologizing for being so distracted. She wagged her tail and nodded at him as if to accept. Things were so much simpler here. Telling Bruce he no longer intended to hand over his pay was not going to be easy. But he had to stand up to the man once and for all—to stand up for what was right.

Levi decided that if he had any chance at making it on his own, he would need the pay he would earn through the harvest to start his own life away from Bruce. He was grateful that his job came with room and board along with a generous wage. He'd done the math, and at the end of the harvest, he would have enough to get himself a small apartment in town. Then he could get another job and maybe think about going back to school. He would love to be like the Amish and live off the land, but he wasn't in any position to acquire any land at this time. Levi had made up his mind that if Bruce ever got his hands on the stolen money, he wanted no part of it. Even if it meant he would struggle, he would earn his money honestly.

Levi exited the barn with a pail of milk for the house. Nettie was already hanging wash on the line, and from the look of the horizon, she probably wouldn't get much done before it rained. Levi said a quick prayer for the community that it would be a slow-moving storm so the women would get their wash hung and dried first.

"Levi," Nettie called to him. "Would you mind going into town when you finish the morning chores? Hiram has a list of things that need to be bought from the hardware store, and I could use a few kitchen staples from the grocery store."

"*Jah,* I'll be happy to."

Nettie picked up the laundry basket and followed him inside the house. "Will you drop off these dishes to Rachel at the bakery on your way out? She left them here after the meal yesterday, and she'll probably need them."

Levi nodded, trying not to seem too eager for the opportunity to see Rachel again so soon.

೫೮೧೪

Levi steered the open buggy into the parking area behind the bakery. Rachel opened the back door and pushed a pile of dirt out the door with a homemade corn broom. She waved to him and smiled as thunder rumbled from a distance. Levi hoped he could get his errands finished before it rained— especially since he had taken the open buggy to save time. It was smaller and easier for the mare to pull. Not to mention easier for Levi to maneuver. His driving skills were improving, but he preferred the smaller buggy.

Levi stepped out of the buggy and gathered the dishes in his hands. He walked toward the back door that Rachel had left open for him. He found her standing at the sink filling a mop bucket with soapy water. She looked so beautiful—even with a dark blue scarf on her head. She wore an old, brown work dress, and her cheeks were a little pink from the heat. But Levi even found the light mist of sweat on her brow to be cute. She turned off the water and went to lift the over-sized bucket from the sink.

Levi rushed up beside her. "Let me get that for you."

Rachel took the dishes from him and stood back, watching with amusement showing on her up-turned lips as Levi struggled with the large pail of water. "Do you usually use this much water to mop the floors?"

He set the bucket down with a small splash.

"*Nee*. I have to mop both the front of the bakery and the kitchen. I thought it might be easier if I filled the bucket to the top rather than filling it twice. I don't like having to change the water."

Levi stood up straight, and then leaned back with a hand at the small of his back to stretch it. "I don't think you should try that on your own. That ten-gallon pail is very heavy when it's full."

Rachel giggled. "Why do you think I let you lift it out of the sink? The last time I tried that on my own, it sloshed all over the kitchen floor and it took me over an hour to mop it all up."

Levi put a hand to his chin. "I would have used that broom to push all the water out the back door."

Rachel narrowed her eyes. "You think you're so smart, don't you?"

"Mmm-hmm." Levi couldn't help but let out a hardy laugh.

"Are you going to stand there and laugh at me, or are you going to help me as long as you're here?"

Levi held his hand in front of his mouth to hide the snicker that threatened to escape. She looked so adorable with her hands on her hips, trying to act tough.

"I can for a few minutes, but then I'll have to go. I need to go into town to pick up a few things before it rains."

Rachel's eyes lit up. "Do you mind if I tag along? I'm out of a few spices and I need fifty pounds of sugar."

"I brought the open buggy. What if it rains? All your sugar will melt."

"I have a plastic tub with a lid we can take to carry it in."

Levi nodded toward the mop bucket. "Is this something you can do when we get back, or can you mop quickly?"

Rachel grabbed the mop. "I can make faster work of it if you'll move the tables and chairs up front."

Levi moved to the front of the bakery and did what Rachel needed. He thought he would probably do almost anything for her.

CHAPTER 23

Bruce Monroe stood outside his motel room leaning against the doorway smoking a cigarette. He looked up the road at the sound of horses hooves against the wet pavement. Laughter filled the stagnant air that hung thick with humidity from the short-lived down-pour. The rain hadn't lasted more than a minute, but that had been long enough to irritate Bruce. The sound of the rain pelting the tin roof of the motel had sufficiently disturbed his sleep so that he couldn't return to the dream he'd been having. Too bad his dream of finding the million dollars had only been a dream. It was enough to put him in the sourest of moods.

Bruce wiped the sleep from his eyes, trying to focus on the young Amish couple running into the hardware store down the road. If he didn't know any better, he'd say that Amish boy was his son. He'd been holding hands with the girl as they ran into the store. Flicking the cigarette onto the pavement, Bruce snuffed it out with his shoe and took off toward the hardware store to see for himself.

As he neared the hardware store, he tried to think of an excuse to enter the store. Luckily, he didn't need one. The couple ran out of the store laughing and holding hands. It was his son alright.

So my boy has found himself a girl. That might come in handy later. If he decides to back out of our little arrangement, I'll threaten to tell the girl everything.

Bruce ducked into the doorway of the business next to the hardware store so he wouldn't be seen. Not that his boy was paying any attention to anything other than *his* girl. Bruce watched his son pull the buggy away from the building and head in the opposite direction. He wondered where they were going next, but it didn't matter. It was obvious to him that he'd forgotten all about the deal they'd made.

I might just have to give him a reminder when I see him on Saturday. I'm not waiting around anymore while he plays house with that girl.

ೲഝ

Rachel opened the umbrella and held it over the top of her and Levi as they left the outskirts of town. What started off as a little bit of drizzle had turned into heavy downpour. Levi didn't want to push the horse to go faster on the slippery shoulder of the main road.

"Maybe taking the open buggy wasn't the best idea I've had." Levi apologized.

Rachel giggled, causing the umbrella to fall away from their heads briefly. "Where is your sense of adventure, Levi Schrock?"

Hearing the name from her lips sounded wonderful. If only there was a way to make it his true identity. Being here with her in the rain was like a dream come true. If only it could last.

"I think I left my sense of humor back at the hardware store. Should we go back and get it?"

Rachel laughed even harder. Levi joined her. He hadn't played in the rain since he was a child, but he had to admit it was more fun with Rachel. He pulled the buggy over into the abandoned schoolyard. He steered the horse toward a set of trees hoping to give the mare a little rest from the heavy rain.

"We don't have much further to go, are you sure you want to stop?"

Levi turned to her and took her hand, leading her out of the buggy. "I want to play in the rain. You can stay under the umbrella where it's safe if you want to, but I'm going to get soaked."

Rachel tossed the open umbrella into the back of the buggy over the plastic tub full of sugar and joined Levi out in the open field. She twirled with her arms outstretched and her face pointed toward the heavens. Levi stopped to watch her. If it was possible, she was even more beautiful with her hair soaked and sticking to the side of her face. Her *kapp* had come loose from her head and hung down her back by the small bow that was tied at the end of the ribbons. She pulled the pins loose and shook her head from side to side until her long hair flopped against her cheeks with a wet slap.

Rachel stopped suddenly and faced Levi. "Why are you staring at me?"

Levi closed the space between them, raindrops forcing him to blink frequently. "Because you're beautiful."

Rachel blinked away raindrops and smiled. Levi pulled her into his arms and pressed his lips to hers. She responded with a quiet moan as he deepened the kiss. With his free hand he ran his fingers through her wet hair, holding her head in place as he continued to kiss her. Rachel folded her arms around his neck, pulling him closer to her. Her breathing was heavy, and she felt light-headed. It was exhilarating. If she wasn't already falling in love with him, she certainly was now.

Levi couldn't believe his luck. Not only was he holding and kissing the girl he had learned to love, she was kissing him back. Was it possible she loved him too? Or was he only dreaming?

CHAPTER 24

Levi lurched forward in his bed, his arms tangled in the freshly laundered linens. His heart raced as he forced himself away from the pull that the nightmare had on him. Rachel had ridiculed him in the dream, telling him she never wanted to see him again. She'd called him a liar.

Taking a deep breath to calm himself, Levi looked out his window at the moon that still hung high in the sky. He couldn't have been asleep very long.

What was I thinking, kissing Rachel this afternoon? She is going to hate me when she finds out I've lied to her. And Hiram will surely fire me!

Levi pressed his weary head back against his pillow. He faced the window, looking out at the moon and wondering how he was going to break the news to Rachel. He would certainly have to wait until after his visit with Bruce on Saturday. He needed closure with his dad before he could move forward with the life he intended for himself. A life that would be free from lies and petty crimes.

Levi sighed, wondering if his life could ever be that simple. He had a feeling Bruce wouldn't let him go without a fight. The man needed him to steal for him or get odd jobs to support him. But maybe if Bruce had the million dollars he would leave him alone forever. He could only hope.

The trouble was, how could he get his hands on a map that might not exist? Did he dare press Abby further for more information? Or worse; did he have the guts to ramshackle thru her house when she wasn't home? No, he could never do anything that disrespectful to his own family.

Stealing small things here and there, or pick-pocketing was a lot different from breaking into someone's house. Not only was the risk greater, he was determined to put his stealing days behind him. He'd spent many hours praying over the last few weeks, asking forgiveness for past crimes and begging God for a way to put an end to any future crimes his earthly father would expect him to commit. If he was to truly change, he had to turn his back on anything and anyone who would threaten his redemption—and that meant his own father.

Levi was afraid to be on his own. Especially if he lost his job with the Miller's.

Lord, I don't have a high school diploma or even any money to go out on my own. Bless me with the tools to change my life even without those things. Please soften Hiram's heart for me and keep him from firing me. Bless my relationship with Rachel to honor you in every way. I love her, and I don't want to lose her. Give me the courage to tell her and Hiram the truth about who I am. Give them understanding hearts for me, Lord. Heal Hiram and make him strong again. Bless him with long life.

Levi closed his eyes intending to continue his prayer, but he fell back asleep. When he woke again, it was morning. He could hear the rooster crowing out near the barn. Levi's stomach growled, telling him he was just as hungry as that rooster must be. He pushed his aching body from the bed and stretched for a minute. He could smell coffee, which meant Nettie had been up for a while already. He had tried to rise before her nearly every day since he'd arrived, but it seemed she awoke earlier each morning. He dressed quickly so he could get to the milking before Nettie or Hiram went out there after tiring of waiting for him. The sun was barely up, but he'd already learned that the day began when the farm was ready—not when the farmer decided.

As he trailed down the stairs, the smell of cooking bacon made his mouth water. He knew he had at least thirty minutes worth of chores to do before he could get any breakfast. He would get the milk for the house first before he did anything to ensure Hiram would have some fresh milk when he sat down to eat with Nettie. They had been so good to him, and he would miss them when he had to leave, which might be sooner than he'd originally anticipated if he went through with his plan to tell the truth at the close of the week.

"*Gudemariye,* Levi. Would you like some *kaffi* to take with you before you head out to the barn?"

"*Danki*," he said as he took the steaming mug from her hands. "I'll be back with the milk before Hiram comes down for breakfast."

Nettie smiled and nodded as she went back to stirring a large iron skillet full of eggs.

Levi left the kitchen before his hunger made him forget his manners. He was tempted to snitch a piece of bacon off the plate, but he forced himself out the door into the humid morning air.

His walk to the barn was filled with the sound of birds chirping and flitting about the trees. Nettie had put out some fresh bird seed in the feeder, and the rain had filled the bird bath with fresh water for their morning routine. He would have loved to spend a few minutes watching them, but he had a job to do. His strong back was the only thing he had going for him for the time-being, and he wasn't about to waste time on bird-watching. If he wanted a chance to keep his job after he told Hiram the truth, he would have to prove to the man that his services were indispensable. Hopefully, his hard work would speak for itself when the time came.

CHAPTER 25

Rachel woke with a stiff neck, most likely from playing in the rain. *Mamm* had always told her to keep dry and warm or she would catch a cold. She felt awful and she ached all over. But she felt her time with Levi was worth every ache. Perhaps some of *Mamm's* herb tea would help ease her muscles back into shape. She hadn't slept well, but most of that was because of the giddiness that filled her from head to toe. She'd decided hours ago that she was definitely in *lieb* with Levi. When she entered the large kitchen, her *mamm* was busy at the stove making a fresh pot of *kaffi*. Rachel cleared her throat and corralled her emotions so as not to give away her feelings to her *mamm's* watchful eye.

She shuffled up next to her *mamm* and put the tea kettle on, ignoring the cup in front of her. "I need tea this morning, *Mamm*. I feel a little stiff from being caught in the rain yesterday when Levi took me into town to get sugar for the bakery."

She'd dried off for the most part before reaching home for the day, but she was certain her *mamm* had noticed her rumpled clothing and disheveled hair.

Lizzie looked at her *dochder* and smiled. "I sort of noticed something was different, but I didn't want to offend you. You've been spending quite a bit of time with Levi."

She'd been waiting for such a comment from someone in her *familye,* but she expected it more from her *grossdaddi.* But since he was recuperating from a possible heart attack, she'd thought she was in the clear.

"We've become friends. I've spent more time with *Grossdaddi* and Nettie since he's been ill, and Levi is always there. He offered to give me a ride into town since he had to run errands for Nettie. But since he took the open buggy, we got pretty soaked in the rain."

Concern showed on Lizzie's face. "I hope you were able to salvage the sugar from melting."

That was all she was concerned about? Rachel knew her *mamm* trusted her to make smart decisions, but would it really be that easy to participate in her *rumspringa* without her *mamm* looking over her shoulder? She'd never given her parents any reason to worry or question her judgment, but this was a first time a boy had entered the equation.

"*Jah,* I brought a plastic tub with a lid just in case."

The tea kettle began to whistle, and Rachel took some tea out of the glass jar and put it in the small steeping basket. Dropping it into her cup, she removed the kettle from the flame and poured the hot water over the tea, using the little chain to bob the aluminum basket up and down in the water. She sat down at the kitchen table and spooned two teaspoons of sugar into the cup and held the steaming beverage to her lips to blow on it.

Lizzie sat down across from Rachel. "I hope you don't get a cold from playing out in the rain like that."

Rachel nearly spit her tea across the table at her *mamm.* "Who said I was playing in the rain?"

Lizzie smiled knowingly. "You did. Since I just took you on Saturday to pick up sugar, I'd say you wanted to go into town because of the company."

Her *mamm* knew her all too well. But she was smiling. Was it possible she didn't care that her youngest *dochder* was taking a beau? Rachel's cheeks heated at the thought of it. She couldn't look at her *mamm,* so she kept her face down blowing and sipping on her tea.

"We've become friends."

Lizzie smiled wider. "You already said that."

Rachel pursed her lips. "I wasn't certain that you heard me."

"He seems like a nice young *mann.* Your *grossdaddi* and Nettie tell us he's a hard worker."

It delighted Rachel that her *familye* liked her new beau. She would never admit to them her interest in Levi beyond friendship, but she suspected her *mamm* already knew.

The hot tea began to work on relaxing Rachel's stiff muscles. She could no more regret the stiffness any more than she could regret her time with Levi the day before. She had a long day ahead of her, but one look out the window at the myriad of colors painted across the sunrise, and she knew the day held promises that would come with no regrets.

Rachel tipped the cup and emptied the last drops down her throat. They felt soothing going down, and would help her to do her chores before work. She had to gather eggs and milk Daisy before she could go. She needed the ingredients for her day, and her *mamm* needed them to start breakfast for the *familye.*

She brought the eggs in quickly and rushed out to the barn to get enough milk to fill a few Mason jars. While her *mamm* made breakfast, she would feed the chickens and then rush inside to change her dress for the day ahead of her. Thankfully, her *daed* and *bruder* would finish the rest of the chores.

As she scattered chicken feed along the ground for the pecking hens, her mind drifted to Levi and the kisses they'd shared in the rain. It was her first experience with a real kiss, and it had left her wanting more of the same. She wanted to kiss Levi every day, but she wasn't sure if he would want to after the way he suddenly pulled away from her at the end of their time together. He'd made an excuse that he didn't want her to catch a cold, but there had been something in the way he'd looked at her that told her there was more to it than that. What had he wanted to say to her that he'd kept to himself?

CHAPTER 26

By the end of the week, Levi knew without a doubt that Rachel loved him and that he returned her feelings for him. They had met each night at the dock of the B&B, and had talked and kissed late into the night. Rachel had voiced a desire to explore the *Englisch* world during her *rumspringa*. Levi hoped it would work out for them when she discovered he was an *Englischer*. He decided that tonight would be the night to tell her the truth. Then in the morning, instead of taking Bruce his weekly wages, he would sever his ties with him, and he would be a free man.

Levi patted Lulu's side as he sat down on the small stool to prepare for the morning milking. When the large pail was full, he patted Lulu once again, thanking her for cooperating with him.

A noise from the loft of the barn drew his head automatically toward the rustling sound. Bruce staggered toward the edge of the loft, kicking alfalfa hay to the floor of the barn below him. Levi's heart lurched in his chest as he stood abruptly, knocking over the small stool and causing Lulu to let out a nervous *moo*.

Levi rushed to the edge of the loft and looked up at Bruce, who was standing dangerously close to the edge. "What are you doing here?"

Bruce waved his half-empty bottle of whiskey in one hand and held the other arm out in mock-balance. "I've been here a couple of days, but now my food is gone and my last bottle is half empty. I need some breakfast. Be a good boy and get your dad something to eat."

Levi's lips formed a grim line. "What happened to the motel room I paid for?"

Bruce plopped down on the edge of the loft and let his legs dangle precariously over the edge. "They kicked me out when I ran out of money to pay for the room. I told you that money you gave me wasn't enough to pay the bills."

Levi stood under his father, prepared to catch him if he toppled over the edge of the loft. "It would have been enough if you would have budgeted the money instead of spending so much on cigarettes and whiskey."

Taking a swig from the whiskey bottle in his hand, Bruce leaned over the edge of the loft, making Levi very nervous. If the man fell, he might break a few bones in the best-case scenario, and then he would have a tough time convincing Hiram of his worth as a farm-hand. He would have a hard time explaining Bruce's presence to his boss.

"Why don't you come down from there and we'll talk. I'll get you something to eat, and then I'll take you back into town and get you back into the motel."

Levi didn't want to spend his hard-earned money on this man anymore since all he did was waste it on booze and cigarettes. But if it would buy him the time he needed until he could explain things to Rachel and Hiram in his own way, it might be worth it.

Bruce pushed himself to his feet and teetered for just a second, causing Levi to feel a rush of adrenaline course through his veins.

Taking a step back, Bruce waved the bottle at his son again. "My things are up here. I'll go sit with them. Bring me something to eat, and then we'll talk."

Levi wrung his hands. "It might be a while before I can sneak any food out of the house without the Millers knowing. They'll be sitting down to eat in just a few minutes. I can't just walk in there and take a plateful of food out of the house when they're sitting right there."

Bruce frowned. "Well you better hurry up Boy, or I'll come in there after it. I'm hungry."

Levi felt like a kid again, cowering under his dad's authority. The last thing he needed was to have Bruce barge into the Miller's house and frighten them. There would be no time for a plausible explanation then.

"I'll get you the food, but I need you to be patient. Promise me you'll stay put until I get back."

Bruce raised his upper lip, exposing his teeth like a rabid dog. "I ain't promising you nothing, Boy.

You hurry on into that house and fetch me some breakfast, or I'll be coming in after it. And while I'm in there I might just tell your boss exactly who you are."

Levi found it difficult to pull enough air into his lungs. Was he having a panic attack? If he was, he couldn't let Bruce see his weakness. The cruel man would play off of it, and he would be on the losing end of the game.

Levi clenched his jaw. "I'll be back just as soon as I can. There's no need to threaten me."

Bruce whipped his head around toward Levi so fast, he nearly fell over. "Don't you EVER think you can tell me what to do, Boy. I'm the boss of you, and don't you ever forget that."

Levi leered up at Bruce. "I already have a boss. I need a dad."

He knew he was pushing his luck speaking out of turn the way he was, but he had reached his limit for tolerance of this man.

Bruce waved a hand behind him as he walked toward the back of the loft away from the edge. "Go on. Get out of here. And don't come back without some food for your old man."

Levi took the pail of milk and exited the barn. Hiram's presence just outside the entry surprised him. His heart lurched again, and he wondered if he was too young to suffer a heart attack.

Hiram nodded. "I was just coming out to see if you'd fallen asleep milking Lulu. Nettie has breakfast ready. Might as well eat it while it's hot. The rest of the chores will keep until you finish."

Levi nodded to his boss, fearful the man had overheard his conversation with Bruce.

CHAPTER 27

If Hiram had heard him conversing with Bruce in the barn, his expression didn't show it. Aside from the clanking of a fork on a plate, the room was silent. It wasn't like either of them to be this quiet during breakfast, but Hiram had his nose in the latest issue of *The Budget,* and Nettie was busy eating. Levi picked at his breakfast, moving the eggs around the plate. His melancholy went unnoticed this morning, and he was grateful.

When Nettie rose from the table to get a second cup of coffee, Levi took the opportunity to stuff a biscuit and a few pieces of bacon into his napkin and push it back onto his lap. The tricky part would be to get out of the door with it. Perhaps if he took his time eating, Nettie would start the dishes before he finished, and Hiram would remain glued to his newspaper. With any luck, he would be able to slip out without either of them being the wiser.

Just as he'd hoped, Nettie started to clear the table while he finished his eggs. He grabbed another biscuit and a few more strips of bacon off the plates before she removed them, and poured himself another glass of milk. He was hungry, but he was nervous.

Paranoid was probably more likely. He took Hiram to be the type of man to say outright if there was something on his mind. But his silence this morning was a little unnerving.

Levi quickly gobbled down his breakfast, and then picked up his napkin full of food and went for the back door while Nettie's back was turned. He'd already thanked her for the meal, so there would be no reason to linger. As his hand went for the door handle, Hiram called his name. He tried to turn around without showing the napkin he held close to him.

"How's the corn looking this week?"

Levi smiled with pride, knowing he had helped the plants grow by tending to them. "The ears are getting mighty thick. We should be ready to start picking the first few rows this week."

"I'd like you to take a bushel of tomatoes and squash up to the roadside stand today. There is a *gut* breeze to keep you cool today. Should be a *gut* day to sell to *Englischers* passing by the main road. If that corn is as thick as you say, then take a bushel of that up there and sell it too. The prices for vegetables and the change jar are on the shelf in the tack room. I'll walk up there in a little while and sit with you if you want me to."

Levi could feel the heat rising to his cheeks.

"That isn't necessary. I wouldn't want you to strain yourself too soon."

Hiram waved a hand at him. "Doctor Davis said I need to start walking every day. The end of the road is a *gut* start, don't you think?"

"Jah. I'll see you in a little while then."

Levi rushed to the barn. He had to act fast if he was going to get his dad out of the barn and get the vegetables picked and hauled to the roadside stand under the big oak tree on the main road before Hiram took his walk out there to meet him.

First things first; he climbed the ladder to the loft, and thankfully, found his dad asleep in the alfalfa hay. How long would he sleep? Levi hoped it would be long enough to pick the vegetables and get them back to the barn. He intended on using the enclosed buggy to smuggle Bruce out of the barn. He would put the vegetables in back with the man, and then take him as far as the main road. Bruce would have to walk the rest of the way back to town, which Levi guessed he'd already done when he came here. He set the napkin full of food next to his dad's head and slid down the ladder. Gathering the bushel-baskets, he headed out to the field.

Once there, he picked as quickly as his hands would work, pushing the basket along with his foot while he used both hands to check each ear before removing them from the stalk. In his frantic state, he knew he couldn't keep up this lie any longer. It was eating away at his peace and stealing his joy. Joy that he should be feeling about his love for Rachel. Instead, he was anxious and full of regret. Would this feeling ever go away? He hoped so, or he would surely make a mistake, and at this point, he couldn't afford to do such thing.

With Bruce safely in the back of the buggy with the produce, Levi steered the mare to the end of the road. He parked the buggy under the tree behind the stand to give the horse relief from the sun. He would ask Hiram to take the buggy back with him when he arrived.

Tying the horse to the oak tree, Levi opened the back door and ushered Bruce out. He handed him fifty-seven dollars and grabbed his duffel bag from the back. "This should get you back into the room at the motel for the night. You can use the rest to get yourself some dinner. After that, you're on your own."

Bruce gritted his teeth and growled. "What do you mean *I'm on my own?*"

Levi took in a deep breath. "I mean, I'm out. I can't do this anymore. These people have been very kind to me, and I won't continue to work with you. They don't know where the stolen money is. That is, even if it exists. The authorities haven't been able to find that money all these years. What makes you think you can find it? I won't hurt these people, and I won't let you hurt them either."

CHAPTER 28

Bruce caught Levi off guard and pushed him up against the tree by his neck. His fingers dug into the flesh of Levi's neck, and he struggled to bring in air.

"What are you gonna do, Boy? You aren't gonna threaten me. I'm the boss of you. I already told you that." Bruce tightened his grip on his son's neck and knocked his head against the tree. "I'm gonna tell you how it is and you're gonna listen or you're gonna get what's coming to you. I'm gonna give you until tomorrow to deliver that map to me, or I'm gonna take matters into my own hands, and you're not gonna like that. I've been watching you and that pretty little brunette. I'd say by the way she kisses you she likes you a lot. If you don't get me that map, we'll see how much she still likes you when I tell her what kind of a man you really are—a thief and a criminal just like me."

Levi had only stolen under his dad's instruction, and by his way of thinking, he'd been a victim of poor parenting. He'd hated it when Bruce made him steal. The very clothes on his body had been stolen off the clothesline of an Amish farm in

Ohio. He knew he would be held accountable for what he'd taken, but he would not put Rachel in harm's way because of his sins. He was nothing like Bruce, and he wanted nothing more to do with him.

"Now, do we understand each other?"

Levi nodded.

Bruce let him go, and Levi coughed and held his sore neck. He had no intention of helping Bruce. His plans had now changed. He would tell Rachel the truth when they met for their date this evening. Then he would tell Hiram after he finished his work for the day. He would leave the community of his own accord and hope that his final week of pay would be enough to get him as far away from Bruce and all the hurt of losing Rachel. He didn't want to tell her or Hiram the truth, but he owed them that much. He could go away quietly and neither would be the wiser, but that was not the kind of man he wanted to be. If being honest and honorable would come with the price of losing his job and the girl he loved, then that's the price he was willing to pay.

Hiram pulled his straw hat down over his eyes to shield the sun so he could get a better look at what was going on with Levi and the older gentleman. They seemed to be having some sort of scuffle. Hiram didn't know whether to holler at them to make his presence known, or just continue walking toward them at a slow pace. He wished he had the energy to walk faster or even run, especially since it appeared that Levi was in some sort of trouble with the

Englischer. Had the *mann* been so unsatisfied with the quality of the produce, or did Levi know him? Hiram supposed it was possible that the *mann* was attempting to rob Levi, but there wouldn't have been enough time for the *buwe* to have made enough sales to accumulate the money that would make a robbery a worthy attempt.

He was still too far away to know for certain what the apparent argument was about, and it wasn't possible for him to hear their conversation. Hiram remained hidden from their view, thanks to the many trees that lined the long driveway that led out to the main road. Before he was able to get any closer, the *Englischer* picked up a bag from the back of Hiram's buggy and took off walking down the road.

Hiram held back for a moment now that Levi was no longer in any immediate danger. He watched the young *mann* unload the remaining produce onto the stand as though nothing had happened. Had the *Englischer* been the same *mann* that Hiram had heard talking to Levi earlier that morning in the barn? He decided to slow his pace more than was necessary to allow the *Englischer* time to walk down the road and out of sight, and to allow Levi a little space before he approached him.

Levi picked up the cell phone that Bruce had tossed at his feet. Bruce had warned him to answer it when he called tomorrow, but Levi had no intention of doing that. Levi intended only to carry out his own plans for a change. A plan that would put him on a Greyhound bus back to Ohio in search of the aunt he'd never known. Rachel had told him about her, explaining to him that Abby had found the woman a few years ago when she visited the area. Levi knew the woman's name and general location, and that was good enough for him. He prayed that she would take him in like she'd done for Abby until she got a job and her own place. If he had a relative that kind, he would do everything he had to in order to make his life right. He was prepared to do whatever it took to turn his back on the life of crime his dad had forced him into. With the fact that he was about to turn eighteen, he knew that he could be put in jail the way Bruce had so many times. Levi's belief was that there wasn't anything in this world worth going to jail for.

Levi shoved the cell phone in his pocket as Hiram came into view. He was still several yards away, but he instinctively looked up the road to be sure Bruce was no longer visible. Relived at not seeing him, he greeted Hiram cheerfully.

CHAPTER 29

Hiram decided to give Levi time to tell him about the strange visit from the *Englischer* when he was ready. He'd suspected something was amiss, but when he'd gotten confirmation that there was indeed a Levi Schrock from the Ohio community, he'd thought the young *mann* had told him the truth. But after overhearing part of a disturbing conversation between Levi and the *Englischer* earlier, Hiram decided to take a second look at the records he'd received from the Bishop in Ohio. He'd noticed inconsistencies with Levi's story, and now, his confrontation with the *Englischer* confused Hiram. So had the part of Levi's story about living in town with only his *daed,* and having no *mamm* or siblings. According to the records from that community, Levi Schrock was one of the youngest of nine *kinner,* and both his parents resided in the *haus.*

Hiram trusted Levi to come to him with the truth in his own time, and so he let the matter drop for the time being. He'd watched Levi from the window since he'd become ill, and he was a hard worker. He'd always proved he could be trusted. But there was one thing that nagged at the back of Hiram's mind.

Was Levi an *Englischer?*

୫୦୯ଓ

Levi cleared his throat nervously several times, pacing the length of the dock, waiting for Rachel. His palms were drenched with nervous sweat, and his heart raced to the rhythm of the cricket's fast song. He'd rehearsed his speech several times on the way to his meeting with her, so he knew exactly what he wanted to say. It would be those first few words that would be the toughest to speak, but he was determined to see it through, even if it meant he would lose her. He would rather lose her in the truth than keep her in his web of lies.

"Do you always pace nervously when you're waiting on me, Levi?"

His heart sped up at the sight of her. She'd left her hair down, and she'd never been more beautiful than she was now. Rachel closed the space between them and lifted her head to press her lips to his. He tasted the sweetness of her lips. Did he have the right to kiss her one last time? Or should he stop her before they got lost in the moment? He would give almost anything right now if he didn't have to break the news to her, but he'd prayed all afternoon that his announcement would not break her heart. He wasn't certain he could live with himself if he hurt her in any way. He loved her, that he knew, and holding her was only going to make things harder on both of them.

Rachel dropped her arms to her sides and stopped kissing him. "You're doing it again."

Levi looked at her quizzically.

"The other day I felt you pulling away from me, and now I feel it again. Is there something wrong? Have you changed your mind about me?"

Levi swallowed the lump in his throat. This was going to be harder than he thought. He didn't want her thinking he was rejecting her. There was no turning back now. She'd given him the out, and now he had to take it.

"Levi, what's wrong? You can tell me."

He took a deep breath and let it out, turning toward the pond and looking out over the expanse of the calm water. The surface was so smooth it looked like glass in the reflection of the moonlight.

"That's part of what's wrong."

"What's part of it?" Rachel interrupted.

She is not going to make this easy, is she?

"My name is not Levi Schrock, and I'm not Amish."

Rachel smiled, thinking she'd play along with his joke. "Then who are you?"

He cleared his throat. "My real name is Blake Monroe and I'm English—an *Englischer.*"

Tears filled Rachel's eyes and she backed away from him. "If you're an *Englischer,* why did you come here pretending to be Amish? Did you think that was the only way you would be hired to work on the farm? We have plenty of *Englischers* who work with us during harvest season and they assist with barn-raisings. Are you mocking us?"

She was not going to make this easy for him. He'd expected nothing less, so he pressed on. He was shaking, but he needed to press through before he lost his nerve.

"Bruce, my dad, sent me here to get something from your sister Abby, my cousin."

Rachel's eyes grew wide. "You're Abby's cousin? I kissed you!"

Blake tried to comfort her, but she pulled away.

"You and I are not related. Only Abby and I are because our dads were brothers. She is your half-sister."

Rachel moved to the end of the dock and sat down, inviting Blake to join her. "I don't understand. Why wouldn't you just ask your cousin for help instead of going through all this trouble to try and fool us? I feel humiliated. Do you even like me, or is that a lie too?"

Blake turned to her. He wanted to kiss her pouty mouth so badly. He wished he could wipe her tears away. Knowing he'd caused them made his heart sink.

"Of course my feelings for you are real. I love you, Rachel. Nothing will ever change that."

She looked over at him. She could see the sincerity in his eyes. She loved him too, and she owed it to him to listen to his reasons. Rachel leaned her head on his shoulder. He let out a sigh of relief and continued his story.

"Bruce had the idea that if I could come here and work as a hired-hand, that I could keep him at the local motel while I worked on getting information out of Abby. He thought she might be more inclined to spill her guts to a total stranger before talking to someone who was related to her real dad. We'd heard she never knew him and that her mother—your mother—had run from him before she gave birth to your sister."

"*Jah,* that's all true, as far as I know. But since she never met her real dad before he died, why is it so important for you to get information about your *daed's* brother from Abby? She never knew him."

Blake put his arm around Rachel. "I thought as much and told Bruce that was probably the case, but he gets all riled up when he drinks. He's not been a good parent to me. He's been a poor example—teaching me to lie and to steal since I was real little. I've prayed a lot and asked forgiveness, but I need to know that you forgive me too."

"That depends."

Blake held his breath for a moment. "On what?"

"Do you want to become Amish? Do you plan on joining the church?'

Blake sighed loudly. "I'd like nothing more, but I don't think Bruce is going to be too willing to just let me stay here. What happens when your grandfather and the rest of the community finds out I've been lying to them?"

Rachel smiled warmly. "I told you. We are a peaceful and forgiving people. Occasionally we have a trouble-maker in the bunch, but that is true with any group of people. They will forgive you and welcome you the same as they do now."

CHAPTER 30

Rachel sat quietly next to Blake. She hadn't really answered him, and she knew he was waiting. Part of her was hurt that he'd not trusted her with the truth. Another part was angry over being lied to and made a fool of. But most of her loved him.

"It is the way of our people to forgive. But that doesn't mean I will stand by and let you lie to me again."

Blake's heart fluttered happily. He was forgiven, but he would do everything to earn back her trust.

"Thank you. It means everything to me that you forgive me."

"I'm curious about something. Is your *daed* mean to you, Lev--*Blake*?"

His real name sounded strange coming from her lips. Blake swallowed hard as he nodded. He was embarrassed by his answer, but Rachel deserved to know the whole story. "He forced me to steal and threatened me that if I didn't get his important papers from Abby, I was going to pay. How can I go back to him empty-handed? I'm afraid my only choice is to leave here and find a safe place where he won't know where I am. I will have to start a new life there, but at least I won't have to live a life of crime anymore."

"What if you make him *think* you're leaving here? Then you can stay here after telling him some odd destination. Would he fall for such a trick?"

Blake played with her hair that hung down her back. "He might. But he threatened to come here and tell you and your grandfather everything if I don't bring him what he wants."

"What does he want?"

"It's not important. Your sister obviously never knew anything about Eddie Monroe."

Rachel looked up at him. "Is that the only reason you're telling me the truth now? Because your *daed* threatened to tell me?"

"No!" Blake bravely touched his lips to hers.

"I've wanted to tell you since the first time I met you at the bakery. All this lying has given me an ulcer."

Blake found no reason to tell her about the money. It was not an issue and would only worry her. He'd told her the most important thing, and that was his true identity. He'd already made the mistake of saying too much to Abby the first time he'd met her at dinner a month ago. Had he only been in the community a month? It had felt like a lifetime.

"It seems like a lot of trouble to go through just for some papers about his own brother. Was it his Will?"

Blake shook his head. "Something like that. Eddie supposedly left some important papers behind, and Bruce thought he might have given them to Abby before he died."

"The only thing he had with him when he died was a copy of a children's book. *The Velveteen Rabbit.* Eddie's half-sister was given his personal effects when he died. She gave the book to Abby a while back when she visited her in Ohio."

Blake sighed. "Well I guess that settles it then. Bruce will have to go back to Ohio empty-handed. A children's book would be of no use to him. He isn't going to be happy about this. I'm going to have to be very convincing if I want to make him think I'm leaving Indiana too. I like the idea of staying here, but only if your grandfather will let me continue to work for him."

"I'm sure you won't have to worry about that. I must say, *mei grossdaddi* is really quite a clever *mann,* and I have to wonder why he hasn't already figured all of this out for himself. Must be because he's been ill."

Blake shook a little. "Do you really think he might suspect me? I wondered if he'd overheard my conversation with Bruce this morning in the barn."

Rachel gasped. "Bruce was here? He was in *mei grossdaddi's* barn?"

"He spent the night in there last night. Quite possibly more than one night. He's lucky he didn't get caught. Would your grandfather be the type to call the police?"

Rachel giggled. *"Nee.* He would probably invite him in the *haus* for a glass of lemonade."

Blake shook at the thought of it. "That wouldn't be a wise thing to do. Bruce can get a little rough when he's been drinking."

"He wouldn't hurt him would he?" Rachel sounded worried.

"He's bloodied up my lip a few times, but I don't think he's capable of violence. At least I would hope not. But there is no telling what a man is capable of when his thinking is altered with whiskey."

The two of them stood up, and Blake pulled her into his arms. He was happier than he'd ever been, but there was still a big hurdle he had to clear before his life would be at peace.

CHAPTER 31

Bruce struggled to get Rachel into the back of the buggy. It wasn't easy with her hands and feet bound. Her whimpering was getting on his nerves.

"I guess your boyfriend didn't tell you he had a daddy, did he?"

Rachel leered at him with tear-filled eyes. She was angry. Bruce could see it in her eyes. He closed the buggy door and sat in the driver's seat. He pulled on the reins, surprised at how easily the horse obeyed. When he pulled onto the main road, he looked back at Rachel to make sure she was paying attention to him.

"That's right. Your boyfriend came here pretending to be Amish so he could get his hands on the map my brother left to your sister, so we could be rich. You see, right before my brother died, we stole the largest amount of money we'd ever stolen. He was going to stash the money away, and we were going to sit for a while and let the heat cool down before we went back and collected it so we could start spending it. But he crashed your mom's car and died before he could get back with the map. My brother promised me he'd make a map that would mark the money's hiding place. Did my son tell you about the million dollars?"

Rachel's heart sank. Levi—Blake had not told her about a map or a million dollars of stolen money. She'd been such a fool to think he loved her. He only wanted the money—the money he expected Abby to find for him. If she'd had a map from Eddie, she would have said so before now.

Unless she doesn't know she has it! What if it's in the book somewhere? It could be hidden. But how can I tell this mann with tape on my mouth?

Bruce steered the horse down Main Street toward the motel. "I bet you didn't know your boyfriend is a thief *and* a liar. He's quite good at it. He stole the Amish clothes so he could fool all of you into thinking he was just like you. Of course, it was my idea to make him go in under-cover. He wanted to go and meet his cousin like a fool, but I warned him she wouldn't talk to him about it unless she thought she could trust him. That's when I came up with the plan to dress him up like the Amish. He didn't want to because he can be stubborn. But after I gave him a good "talking to", if you know what I mean, he was all for it."

Rachel had an idea she knew exactly what he was talking about. It was obvious this *mann* was far more violent than Blake had let on. Was he even aware that his father was capable of such an act as this? Was it *his* fault she was in danger now? Or was Blake a victim in all of this too? How would she ever be able to trust him again? Or would nothing matter since she would be dead soon?

"How does it feel knowing that your boyfriend fooled you? You didn't really think he actually liked you, did you? His goal was to get his hands on the money the whole time. As soon as your family gets the ransom note, me and my son will be rich. He won't think twice about you when he's counting all his money."

Rachel wept quietly. Her heart was broken and she didn't think she would ever live to see her *familye* again. She knew too much already, and he kept telling her more. He would have no reason to let her go when she could identify him.

Dear Gott, please spare my life. Soften this mann's heart toward me and make him let me go. Give me the courage to forgive him if he should decide to end my life.

ജ്യ

Blake packed his things in the knapsack he'd carried with him when he first came to live with the Miller's. He knew that Bruce would not be convinced that he was leaving Indiana unless he had his things with him, and he knew that man would check his bag. Blake had considered drawing a fake map that would lead his dad on a wild goose chase looking for the money, but Bruce would never believe it. There was no way Blake could make a map to look almost as old as he was. It would take too much time and planning, and he didn't have that kind of time.

Sneaking out of the house with his things, Blake knew it would be easier to get away once it turned dark. The Miller's would be in the sitting room reading from the Bible at this time, just as they had every Saturday night. The sun rested just above the horizon and it was sinking fast. If he didn't get away now while they were preoccupied, he might not get another chance. The walk into town to the motel would take him at least forty-five minutes, and by then, the sky would be pitch-black.

He quickly passed by the bakery and was slightly disappointed to see that Rachel had already left for the day. He'd hoped he could get one last bit of encouragement from her before he faced his father, just in case he walked away with a black eye. He drew comfort from knowing Rachel was safe at home for the night.

CHAPTER 32

"Rachel's been abducted!"

Abby ran through her parent's *haus* looking for Caleb and her *daed*. This was all her fault. If she'd paid closer attention to Rachel, she wouldn't be in jeopardy. She had thought there was something strange about Rachel's new beau asking so many questions, but she'd dismissed it. She'd been too busy with her own life to pay attention to what was going on in her dear *schweschder's* life.

No one was in the *haus*. Odd. Where was everyone? The barn? Abby raced to the barn and threw open the door.

"Daed, where are you? I need your help."

"In here, Abby. *Kume.* We have a new foal."

The sound of her *daed's* voice brought little comfort as she ran to the inner part of the barn where her *familye* sat watching the miracle of life unfold before their eyes. She hated to ruin such a beautiful moment with such tragic news, but it couldn't be helped.

Abby pushed the note she'd found at the bakery into her *daed's* hand. She was out of breath from running, and her face was drenched with tears.

"This note says Rachel's been abducted. The kidnapper is demanding one million dollars, and he thinks I have the map that leads to it. He says I'm to bring him the map or we'll never see her again. Does that mean he plans to...?" Abby couldn't push the unspeakable from her lips. She didn't want to think about the possibility that her *schweschder* could be harmed.

She should have known something was wrong when Levi seemed to know things about Abby's past. Things about Eddie, her real father. She wrote it off as gossip when Levi had said he heard that Eddie had buried a million dollars and left the map to its whereabouts to his only child. That would be her, and she had no such map. She'd not even admitted to Levi that Eddie was her real father.

"*Daed,* I think Levi knows something about this, or he could be in on it. We have to get over to *Grossdaddi's haus* to see what he knows about this. He was asking all sorts of strange questions about Eddie and a million dollars he supposedly hid before he died. Levi said there were rumors around town that he'd left me a map to its whereabouts. I don't have a map to any stolen money."

Caleb jumped into action readying the buggy.

Jacob showed the strain in his eyes. "Why didn't you tell us about this sooner, Abby?"

Abby began to cry all over again. "I didn't think it meant anything. You know how small-town rumors can be. I just didn't think. I'm sorry, *Daed.*"

Lizzie hugged her *dochder* as she wept. "Abby, this isn't your fault. It's mine. If I'd done a better job covering our trail, none of this would have happened. I also knew that she'd been sneaking out late to meet Levi. I didn't think it was a problem since it's her time of *rumspringa.* I was trying to give her some space so she wouldn't leave the community like you and I did, Abby."

"*Mamm,* what if they know about us because I stayed in Ohio all that time? I can't believe it took them this long to catch up to us."

Jacob fought back tears. "We don't know for certain that the two are connected, but if they are, we might have to call the local police to help us find her if we can't get any answers out of Levi."

Hearing that her *daed* thought the police should be called suddenly made it real, and that frightened Abby to her very core. "I'm going with you, *Daed.* This has something to do with me, I just know it."

Jacob didn't argue with his *dochder.* He could see she was determined to go, and she would find a way if he didn't give his consent.

Abby couldn't help but feel guilty for not heeding the warning signs as she climbed into the back of the buggy. Levi had come from a small Amish community in Ohio, just outside of the small town where Abby had grown up. He'd come early for harvest season, and no one had questioned him. He looked Amish, and his story had seemed realistic enough. Her *grossdaddi* had no reason not to bring him on as a hired hand. He was one of their own. Wasn't he?

CHAPTER 33

Blake feared he was probably walking into a beehive at the motel. Bruce was already angry and what he was about to say to him was going to add fuel to the fire. He spent the better part of the walk into town praying and practicing his speech. His legs were sore from all the walking after a long day of farm work, and he wished he'd had a water bottle. The night was balmy, and the Amish clothing was very warm. The only relief he felt was from the slight breeze that cooled his sweaty neck. He pulled off the straw hat and used it to fan his face. If Bruce hadn't given him an ultimatum, he'd have waited until the morning to make this trip into town.

Eager to see Main Street, Blake picked up his pace, kicking up stones along the side of the road. He wished he'd thought to take the buggy and park it on the far end of Main Street because now he would have to walk all the way back, and he was already tired. He hoped that Bruce would take the bait and leave town, but he would have to put on his best poker face to fool the man.

As he approached Main Street, Blake was happy for the street lamps to light his path. All of the stores were closed, and the only traffic was further down where all the fast-food places could be found. The smells coming from them was making him hungry after such a long walk, and he was tempted to keep walking and get himself a burger. It had been a month since he'd had any fast-food. Part of him missed it, but he had to admit Nettie was a fine cook. He had not left the table hungry since he'd been there. He'd suffered hunger too many times with Bruce. As a child, his only saving grace had been the free lunch he got at school.

Blake passed the hardware store, and as he fixed his gaze forward, he saw something that looked out of place. An Amish buggy was parked in front of the motel. Did the Amish ever take a room in a motel, or would they stay with someone in the neighboring community if they were traveling? His heart beat faster as he realized the horse looked a lot like Rachel's.

Blake took off running toward the mare. She recognized him, tipping her head when he approached. He opened the door of the buggy and discovered it was empty. Placing his bag on the seat, he wondered if Rachel had decided to take matters into her own hands and confront Bruce. Not knowing what he would find when he walked into his father's motel room, he walked slowly toward the door. He listened at the door, thinking he heard muffled cries.

"Shut up," he heard Bruce yell.

Shaking, Blake slid over to the window and peered through a small slit in the drapes. His heart slammed to his feet when he saw Rachel bound and gagged. She had been tied to a chair and Bruce had a bottle of whiskey in one hand and a *gun* in the other.

Blake backed away from the window, fearing he would be seen. Then he remembered he'd put the cell phone in the knapsack when he'd packed his things at the Miller's house. He ran over to the buggy, grabbed the phone, dialed three numbers, and then held it to his ear with a shaky hand.

"911, What's your emergency?" the operator on the other end asked.

"My d-dad," Blake stammered. "H-he's kidnapped my girlfriend. He has her tied up in his motel room, and he has a gun! You have to send someone right away."

CHAPTER 34

"What's this all about?" Hiram asked his son-in-law and *grandkinner.*

"We came to see Levi," Jacob said. "Rachel's been kidnapped, and we think he might know where she is."

Hiram nearly fell over at the news. Jacob and Caleb assisted him into the nearest chair.

"Levi went out a little while ago. I thought I heard the door close, so I went upstairs to check on him, he was gone and so were all his things. I looked out the second-story window and saw him walking up toward the main road carrying the same knapsack he showed up here with. I don't know where he could have gone."

"Caleb, go out to the barn and call the police," Jacob ordered his son. "He couldn't have gotten far if he was on foot. Hopefully, they will catch up to him."

"Tell them he was headed toward town," Hiram called after him.

Jacob turned to Hiram. "Will you be alright then? I think we're going to ride toward town to look for Levi. The kidnapper left a note saying that we were to wait for further instructions, but I don't think we can wait. I have to find my *dochder*. When the police get here, give them this note from the kidnapper and tell them we went to look for Levi."

When they left, Hiram took to praying for Rachel's safety. He found it hard to believe that Levi would be involved with kidnapping her.

ॐ

Blake hung up the phone after being assured by the operator that there was an officer already in the area they could send. Knowing the police were probably around the corner, Blake decided he would make an attempt to reason with Bruce. He went to the door of his room and tried the doorknob. It was locked, so he knocked with a shaky hand.

He heard Bruce tell Rachel to shut up again, and then he heard him lean against the door to look through the peephole. The door swung open quickly, and Bruce stood with the gun pointed at his son.

"Well, look who decided to join the party! Get in here before I shoot your girlfriend."

Blake rushed to Rachel's side and knelt down beside her, smoothing her hair. "Are you okay? He didn't hurt you, did he?"

Bruce went over to Blake, picked him up by the back of his shirt, and shoved him across the room.

"Where's my money, Boy?"

Blake held his hands up in surrender. "I don't have it and neither do they. There is no map. There never was one. My cousin never knew her real dad, so there was never an opportunity for him to give her anything."

Bruce cocked the gun in his hand and pointed it toward Rachel. "Don't lie to me Boy, or I'll shoot your girlfriend."

Rachel squealed around the tape that was coming loose on her mouth.

Blake took a few steps closer to Rachel. "I promise you I'm not lying."

Bruce staggered closer, waving the gun carelessly. "I think the two of you planned to run off with my money. I've waited a long time for that money, and I ain't leaving here without *my* money. If I don't get it, I'll shoot the girl."

Blake took another step toward Rachel, keeping his eyes locked on Bruce. "I wish I could give it to you so you'd go away and leave me alone. I don't want to be your son anymore. I haven't for a long time. The truth is, the money doesn't exist, so why don't you just go back to Ohio and let her go."

Bruce gritted his teeth. "You leave me no choice, Son. I have to shoot her."

Bruce aimed the gun at Rachel's head, and Blake dove across her, pushing them both to the ground. The gun went off with a deafening crack, and Blake could feel the hot sting of the bullet piercing his shoulder. Agonizing pain assaulted him just before the room went black…

CHAPTER 35

Blake's ears were ringing, and noises seemed muffled as though he were under water. He blinked a few times, meeting Rachel eyes as they both lay on the floor. They were face-to-face until someone picked her up, chair and all. His eyes closed uncontrollably. Someone had taken her away from him.

ఴల

Rachel looked at Blake, trying to get him to keep his eyes open, but he wouldn't. She wanted to yell his name and tell him to hold on, but her mouth was still taped shut. She could hear Bruce laughing on the other side of the room until the door burst open. Police officers took the gun from Bruce, handcuffed him and hauled him out of the room in one quick movement. One of the officers called for an ambulance from his two-way radio and then approached her.

"Are you okay, Miss?" he asked her.

Rachel looked at Blake lying on the floor, blood pooling around them. He closed his eyes just as the officer lifted her from the floor. She watched as another officer pressed a hotel towel against Blake's wound, while the other removed the tape and ropes that bound her.

Rachel collapsed onto the floor beside Blake. She picked up his hand in hers, held it to her lips and kissed it.

Please, Gott, let him live.

Sirens drew near, and as she looked into Blake's face, she feared he was already dying. He had saved her life, and she might never get the chance to thank him or tell him how much she loved him.

The officer moved Rachel aside as the paramedics lifted Blake onto a stretcher.

"I want to go with him," Rachel said slowly.

The paramedics motioned her to come along.

The officer stopped her. "We'll need a statement from you about what happened here."

"Can it wait? I'm all he has. I need to be with him."

The officer shook his head. "I can give you a ride to the hospital after I get your statement. They'll be taking him directly to surgery, so he won't know you're there."

Rachel stepped away from the officer and followed the paramedics. She turned her head over her shoulder. "He'll know I'm there. You can meet me at the hospital and talk to me while I wait for him."

As Rachel climbed into the back of the ambulance, her *familye* rode up in their buggy.

Abby jumped out and ran to the back of the ambulance. "Rachel, what happened? Is Levi alright?"

"Get the book, Abby. The Velveteen Rabbit. Give it to the police. I think the map is hidden in it somewhere."

ഇരുന്ന

Blake groaned, trying to open his eyes, but his lids felt like they were glued shut.

"Blake, can you hear me?" a sweet, angelic voice asked him.

It sounded like Rachel. If only he could open his eyes. Was he dreaming? Or was he dead? He tried to move, but felt a burning pain in his shoulder that radiated down his arm and across his back.

Dead people don't feel pain, do they?

Blake groaned with pain that seemed to pulsate through his whole upper body. His lips felt dry and his mouth felt pasty. A beeping noise blipped steadily, and the smell of fresh, clean air roused him to wakefulness. Something pinched his nostrils, but he couldn't move his arms to see what it was. A swooshing sound mixed with the beeping. What was that noise? He was sure he'd heard such noises before.

"Blake, are you awake?" the dreamy voice asked again.

Blake fluttered his eyelids. Light peered in through the narrow slit, but he just couldn't seem to pull them open any more than that.

Lord help me. I think I'm dying. Please don't let me die. I have to save Rachel.

Blake moved his head slightly from side to side, testing his eyelids once more. Gradually the light brightened, and the grogginess lifted a little more. A shadow stood over him. It looked like Rachel.

"Rachel," he struggled to say.

He felt the warmth of her hand in his. "I'm here."

Her voice sounded shaky, and he heard her sniffle. Had she been crying?

"Where—am—I?" he managed around the pain.

"You're in Elkhart General Hospital. Can you open your eyes?"

Blake tried his eyes again. They fluttered several times until they focused on Rachel. He blinked, wondering if he was dreaming.

"What happened? I hurt."

Rachel smiled sympathetically. "Your *daed* shot you. Don't you remember?"

"Where—is he?" the struggle to speak sent waves of pain through him.

Rachel looked away. "They took him to jail."

Blake pursed his lips. "Good."

Rachel squeezed his hand lightly. "I'm so sorry."

"It's not—your fault." Blake reached up slowly and grabbed at the nose clasp that fed oxygen through his nose and tried to remove it.

Rachel reached up and replaced it. "Leave this on until the doctor tells you that you can take it off.

You just got out of surgery a few hours ago, and I'm sure you need it."

A nurse walked into the room just then. "I see you're awake. You are one brave young man taking a bullet for this young lady. How are you feeling?"

Blake tried to smile, but gave up. "Not—so—brave anymore."

"You had a bullet wedged in your shoulder. I imagine it will be a few weeks before you'll be ready to save any more damsels in distress." The nurse turned to Rachel. "Be careful. He won't be there to save you if you get yourself into any more trouble."

Rachel smiled at the nurse, hoping she was kidding. "When can he have visitors? *Mei familye* has been here all night waiting to see him."

Blake became nervous. Were they going to reprimand him for lying to them? Or would they be so pleased that Rachel was now safe that they would welcome him? Were they really as forgiving as Rachel had told him when they'd sat on the dock together?

"They can come in one at a time." The nurse said.

"Danki," Rachel said.

She left the room and came back with Abby.

"My *schweschder* tells me we are cousins. I'm very pleased to meet you, Blake. *Danki* for saving Rachel."

Blake nodded. "I'm sorry."

Abby looked at him with tears in her eyes. "I know. I'm more sorry that we didn't get to grow up together. We are *familye,* and since you just lost part of yours, we will be your *familye,* if that is what you want."

Blake felt a tear roll down his cheek. "Yes."

Abby looked at Rachel. "Should we tell him now, or wait?"

Blake strained to look at the two of them. "Tell me—what?"

Abby smiled. "The map was in the inside flap of the book Eddie left me. The police found the money an hour ago. All one million dollars of it. The best part is, they sent an officer here to tell me there is a reward. We each get fifty-thousand dollars, cousin."

Blake tried to shake his head. "You can—have it."

"I won't hear of it, dear cousin. I hear you plan on staying in the community. You will need to buy a piece of land if you plan to be an Amish farmer."

With that, she left the room.

Blake didn't know what he'd done to deserve such a nice cousin. She was the only family he had now, and she had welcomed him as his real self. Not to mention, she'd thought of *him* with regard to the reward money. Though a part of him felt he didn't deserve it, he would welcome it if it meant he would be able to own a piece of God's green earth and work it as his own. God had truly answered his prayer.

A few minutes later, Hiram entered the room and stood next to his bed.

"How long before they let you out of here, Blake?" he asked.

Hearing his name from Hiram made him a little more than nervous. Did the man want him to get well so he could take him out to the barn and have good "talk" with him?

"I—don't know." Blake answered.

"I hope it's soon because we need you for the harvest. That's what I hired you for, and I need a *gut* strong *mann* to help me. I hope you're still willing to help me even though I hear you're a wealthy *mann* now."

Blake couldn't believe his ears.

"I'm not—fired?"

Hiram laughed. It was probably the only time Blake had heard him *really* laugh. "*Nee*, you can't get out of this by getting shot. We know that your *daed* was the one that forced you into this life. You were a victim more than we were."

Blake swallowed the lump in his throat. "I'm sorry."

"I know you are, Son. I forgive you for lying about being Amish, but Rachel tells us you'd like to join the church."

"Yes, I—would."

"Get your rest then, and we'll talk to the Bishop about getting you into the classes as soon as you get out of here. You can take the Baptism after the harvest."

Hiram patted Blake's hand and then left the room. A few minutes later, Rachel returned.

"*Grossdaddi* says you're to take the Baptism in the fall."

Blake chuckled, but the pain stopped him.

"*Jah.* Imagine. Me—Blake Monroe. Amish!"

"It doesn't matter if your name is Blake Monroe, Levi Schrock, or something else. *Gott* knows your heart, and Just so long as it belongs to Him…and me…" Rachel kissed him lightly on the lips.

Blake closed his eyes, feeling overwhelmed with thankfulness. "Always."

Danki, Lord.

Christian Historical Romance
Available on Kindle or Nook

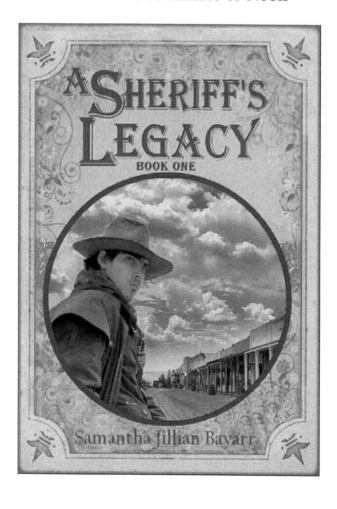